Percival and Hunting Aircraft

R. JOHN SILVESTER

Publication of this book was originally to have been by Nelson & Saunders but as a result of their liquidation before publication, but after the completion of production work, publication is now undertaken by the author:-

R. J. Silvester
47, Lynwood Avenue, Stopsley, Luton LU2 7TY
Telephone: Luton (0582) 23706

Sole distribution by:-
Midland Counties Publications
24, The Hollow, Earl Shilton, Leicester LE9 7NA
Telephone: 0455 47256

ISBN 0 9513386 0 9

© 1987 R. J. Silvester

Editorial production by Kristall Productions,
Surbiton, Surrey, KT6 4AG
Typeset by Qualitext, Salisbury SP2 7BE
and printed by LR Printing Services, Manor Royal,
Crawley, West Sussex RH10 2QN

CONTENTS

Jean Batten poses with her Gull G-ADPR at Gravesend. G-ADPR was one of the most famous of all Percival aircraft. The long-range tank fitted in the cabin of this record-breaking aircraft can be seen together with the sight gauges mounted in the fuel and oil tanks in the centre section and wing (Flight).

FOREWORD

When I was a child, aeroplanes were still very much a novelty. Many ex-pilots of the Royal Flying Corps – later the Royal Air Force – had purchased redundant aircraft, mainly Avro 504s, in which they hoped to entice the general public into sampling this new form of transport and at the same time wrest a living. One day one of these 'barnstormers' landed in a field nearby to ply his trade and, true to form, the populace swarmed there, my parents among them with my younger brother and myself in tow.

From that day onward I became, in modern parlance, an 'aviation freak'. The sound of an approaching aircraft would send me into the garden to eagerly scan the sky! For a long time journeys to school, that bane of childhood, were invariably made with arms outstretched and lips vibrating in an attempt to imitate the sound of an aero-engine.

Life for me, on the whole, was idyllic. My home-town of Luton was strategically placed as far as aerial activity was concerned. It was quite usual to see the olive-green Vickers Virginias growling away across the heavens as they clawed for height so that the airmen perched on the wings could be dragged off by their parachutes. From de Havillands at Hatfield would come Moths, and occasionally Hawker Harts would thrust their purposeful way northwards from their base at Hendon.

From time-to-time the huge bulk of the airship R101 would pass overhead on its way back to its base at Cardington some twenty miles away but in early October 1930 after experiencing engine trouble it flew into high ground on the outskirts of Beauvais in France. In the resulting conflagration all but seven of the sixty-five on board perished. This appalling disaster however had little effect on my enthusiasm for aircraft.

On my seventh birthday my interest was further stimulated when an uncle presented me with a small wire and silk flying model based on the Bleriot monoplane. It was powered by a rubber band which had to be wound up by turning the propeller – usually with a well-bruised index finger. From time-to-time one of the many magazines for boys then published would give away 'free' paper flying models as a promotional gift. When this happened, pocket money was sacrificed to buy a copy. Paper models were most popular at that time; they were ingeniously designed, fairly easy to construct and flew remarkably well.

For the more affluent, ready-made models could be purchased, the most notable being those manufactured by International Model Aircraft under the trade name 'Frog', derived from 'flies rising off ground'. They were beautifully made with pressed aluminium fuselages and formed paper wings reinforced at their roots by metal ribs. Each model came complete in a box incorporating a geared mechanism to wind up the rubber motor. The ultimate model in the range was that of the Hawker Hart, at that time the latest day-bomber aircraft.

From time-to-time Sir Alan Cobham would visit the area with his 'flying circus' which he based at Lewsey Farm, a site now covered by a housing estate. These visits were a highlight and to attend them was essential! A commentator directed the attention of the patrons (through large horns mounted on the top of a van) to items of interest and, during lulls in the programme, extolled all and sundry to sample the joys of flying for the sum of five shillings (25p).

In addition to the big Handley-Page W10, the smaller Airspeed Ferry, a Fox Moth and several two-seat aircraft engaged in pleasure flights were a

This paper model, designed by Mr. Rigby a specialist in this form of model making, was given away as a 'Free' promotional gift with the Modern Boy in 1932. It was obtained for the cost of two issues of the magazine, 4d (about 2p).

number of 'novelty' aircraft, one of which was an Avro autogyro. This, according to the commentator, was the safest aeroplane designed and virtually impossible to crash, the information being given while the machine demonstrated its abilities above. As the autogyro prepared to land the commentator continued his patter. '. . . you have seen its remarkable flying abilities, now watch how easily it lands . . . as safe as houses!' At that point the machine, which had been trundling serenely over the turf, promptly stood on its nose, the rotor blades folding together over its buried propeller as if trying to hide its head in shame!

It would not be fitting to omit that other aeronautical highlight, the Royal Air Force Display held annually at Hendon. This was attended regularly from 1933 until 1937 when it ceased to exist. Everything that happened on the day was assumed to be as planned, even when one of the participants in a 'student and instructor' routine gyrated into the ground after striking a search-light during a low pass!

The purchase of a new bicycle for the princely sum of £2.5.0d. (225p) made it possible to visit places of aeronautical activity previously denied to me. At Dunstable Downs a small group of enthusiasts participated in a new sport, launching their gliders from the top of the hills. Before the innovation of an endless rope system the gliders were hauled to the top of the hill manually, much of the effort being supplied by the enthusiastic onlookers. Participation was also encouraged for the launches made with a long bungee cord hooked at its centre to the nose of the machine.

The willing bystanders, myself among them, would divide equally on each side of the rope and, on the command 'run' given by the pilot, gallop like Gadarene swine toward the brow of the hill, the glider being restrained by two helpers holding the tail. When our lungs were almost bursting and we felt we could run no further, the pilot would shout for the tail to be released and with the wind howling in the bracing wires the glider would shoot over our heads.

It was not until I was fifteen years of age that the ultimate dream of becoming airborne was realised; the opportunity being presented while on holiday with my family at Southsea by the Portsmouth, Southsea and Isle of Wight Aviation Company. They were operating a ferry service to the Isle of Wight, the return fare being fifteen shillings (75p) an opportunity which could not be missed. This introduction to flying increased my determination further to become part of this fascinating aeronautical scene! I resolved to remain at Hayward-Tyler Ltd, the local hydraulic engineering works with whom I had managed to gain employment and bide my time until I was old enough to join the Royal Air Force Volunteer Reserve . . . but that was not to be!

HAWKER-HART MKII Day Bomber

A superb Flying Scale Model of the famous R.A.F. Day Bomber. Incorporates many revolutionary features in design and construction. Spring undercarriage operates in similar manner to the actual aeroplane. Detachable wings. Interplane struts and bracing wires. Triple motor coupled to precision cut gear box. Wing span 19 ins. Average length of flight, 750 feet. Complete with patent high-speed winder box, full equipment and illustrated flying manual.

This advertisement was issued in 1934 by Lines Bros. who were the sole concessionaires for the ready-to-fly model aircraft produced by International Model Aircraft Ltd under the trade name 'Frog'.

Early inspiration . . . the de Havilland Moth was often seen flying over Luton. This particular aeroplane was operated by Aerofilms Ltd which eventually became part of the Hunting Group.

The R101, built by Short Bros at their specially constructed base at Cardington in Bedfordshire, floats from its mooring mast. The ship was destroyed when it crashed near Beauvais, France, in October 1930.

The Westland Wessex of the Portsmouth, Southsea and Isle of Wight Aviation Ltd in which the author made his first flight. It was delivered to the company in 1932 and was specially modified to meet their requirements.

CHAPTER 1

PERCIVAL AND HIS GULLS

In 1937 there appeared in the local paper an advertisement which read . . .
'Wanted, Junior Draughtsman, previous aircraft experience not essential –
Apply Box XYZ.' Being an avid aircraft enthusiast from a very early age it
took but a few moments to work out that Box XYZ applied to the Percival
Aircraft Company that had recently moved from Gravesend to Luton
Airport which was then under construction. It took much longer to compose
a letter of application, but I must have done reasonably well as a few days
later I received an invitation to attend for interview.

On the appointed day, with hair well 'Brylcreemed' in the approved
manner of the time, suit pressed and shoes polished to perfection, I
presented myself at a farmhouse, a legacy from the previous tenants, which
at that time served as offices. I was ushered into a large bedroom that had
been converted into an office and was being used by Mr A. A. Bage who
was, at that time, the Chief Draughtsman. I must have satisfied him during
the short interview (or he must have been desperate for staff) because I was
offered the post at a fabulous salary of 27/6d (137½p) per week, a vast
improvement on the 10/6d (52½p) I was then earning at Hayward Tyler Ltd.
the local hydraulic engineering company. Needless to say, I accepted on the
spot! And so, on a bright Monday morning in March 1937, I joined an
enthusiastic band of aircraft builders, an association which was to continue
for almost twenty-three happy years.

In the halcyon days of aviation between the two World Wars, the name
Percival was synonymous with aviation records. Long before he conceived
the Gull, Edgar Wickner Percival, C.Eng., FRAeS, FIMechE, MSAE, MIAeE,
AFIAeS, MIMarE, FRSA, had achieved much in the field of aviation.

Although born in 1897 at Albury in New South Wales, Australia, his
family had moved at the turn of the century to a large farm on the fertile
river flats of the Hawkesbury at Richmond, NSW. From there he attended
Fort Street High School in Sydney and later the Sydney Technical College
before rounding off his education at Sydney University. With his brothers,
Edgar's early life was spent assisting in the running of the family farm – but
the aviation bug had bitten, for he was an avid reader of any literature
published on the emerging science of aeronautics. He had also constructed
and flown – albeit for short distances – primitive gliders of bamboo and
calico.

When he was fourteen years of age an event occurred which was to have
a profound effect on his future life for it was in 1911 that a young dental
surgeon from Parramatta was given permission to fly aeroplanes from a
large field almost on the boundary of the Percival's farm. The name of that

young dental surgeon was William Ewart Hart who was destined to become the holder of the first pilot's licence issued by the Australian Government. The opportunity that he offered was seized with both hands by young Edgar who spent all his spare time helping with the construction, and later the flying, of the aeroplanes Hart was building. To pursue this activity Percival was allowed 'time off' from an apprenticeship he had gained at a well known Engineering Company in Sydney.

His association with 'Billy' Hart was brought to an end by the outbreak of the First World War. As Percival had had a wealth of experience 'breaking in' horses on the family farm, the eighteen year old Edgar joined the 7th Australian Light Horse and was soon serving in the war zones of the Middle East – but not for long! As soon as the opportunity occurred he transferred to the Royal Flying Corps where, after a nominal tuition of twenty-three minutes duration, he flew solo.

During those desperate days, the life of a pilot flying over the Western Front was measured in hours and the losses over the battlefields of France were reaching alarming proportions. To combat this, Percival and others were sent to England after their first tour of combat duty for further training. After the completion of this, Percival was posted to Number 60 Squadron commanded by the great 'Billy' Bishop VC with whom many combat missions were flown. He was then posted to the Middle East where he became a Founder Member of Number 111 Squadron and served with it until the end of the hostilities.

War or no war, Percival did not allow such trifles to restrict his ability to design aeroplanes or fly them! While serving in Egypt he designed a special aircraft based on the Bristol F2b Fighter powered by a Rolls-Royce Eagle engine. He also undertook all the test flying.

Edgar contended that aerial transportation was ideal for Australia where long distances had to be covered. Furthermore, the climate was almost perfect for this form of transport and there was plenty of open space. Percival resolved to pursue a career in flying, so, when he was demobilised, he purchased three surplus aircraft from the Royal Air Force, two Avro 504s and a DH6 and shipped them back to his home in Richmond. During the war, the field from which he and Hart had flown had been used by a Flying Training School and to accommodate the aircraft a large hangar had been built. As the establishment was, at that time, no longer required for military purposes (although in later years it was to become the New South Wales Base of the Royal Australian Air Force), Percival acquired the lease and for nine fruitful years operated commercially, undertaking aerial surveys, private charter and advertising flying, as well as giving joyrides. At the same time he constructed airscrews and undertook the modification of proprietory aircraft to meet the requirements of their owners.

By nature E. W. P. was a most competitive person – particularly where flying was concerned! A competition had been arranged by the Federal Government in 1926 for locally designed light aircraft, the aim being to test both the pilots and the aeroplanes in all aspects of flying. The challenge was

readily accepted by Percival who entered and flew his co-designed machine. Although up against very professional and stiff opposition (three well-proven aircraft and their very experienced pilots had been specially imported from the United Kingdom) he won some £940 of the £1,000 prize money! Prior to this event he had won many other competitions including the *Melbourne Herald* Air Race of 1923 which was flown from Melbourne to Geelong and back.

With few exceptions, all Governments have tended to be apathetic toward flying, particularly the private aspects, and in 1926 the Australian Government was no exception! This caused Edgar a great deal of frustration and although he had received little or no encouragement from the numerous letters he had written to manufacturers of aircraft in the United Kingdom, he resolved to come here, initially for a period of six months, to establish himself and obtain financial backing. In the event, he never returned to his homeland as a resident but always retained his Australian Citizenship.

Soon after he arrived in England in 1926, Percival was approved by the Air Ministry as a test pilot for seaplanes, flying boats and land planes and for a time undertook 'freelance' test flying. Among the many aircraft he test flew were the Hendy Hobo and the Hendy 302A, both of which were designed by Basil B. Henderson, the latter being flown by Percival in the Kings Cup Air Race of 1930 at an average speed of 121.5 mph.

In addition to test flying, Percival undertook the design of aeroplanes,

The prototype Percival Gull was built by the Lowe-Wylde British Aircraft Company and the fuselage is seen here under construction in their factory at Maidstone (LAT).

the most noteable (prior to those he designed before establishing his own Company) was the Saro-Percival Mailplane. It was, as were his later aircraft, a low wing monoplane of wooden construction. It had a cantilever wing, a single fin and rudder, a fixed undercarriage and was powered by three de-Havilland Gipsy III engines. A single pilot was accommodated in an enclosed cabin ahead of the mail compartment and it was the first aeroplane in the (then) British Empire to carry a payload of 1,000 lb for a distance of 1,000 miles.

It was undertaken as a joint project and built by Saunders Roe Ltd at their works in Cowes on the Isle of Wight with Percival supervising the construction and undertaking all the test flying. A full certificate of airworthiness was issued early in 1932 and the machine was allocated the registration G-ABLI.

Soon afterwards Saunders Roe Ltd was re-organised and Percival sold his interests in the aircraft which was re-designated the Saro A24. Saunders Roe Ltd then established close ties with Spartan Aircraft Ltd (formerly Simmonds Aircraft Ltd) who were also located in Cowes, and it was arranged that they would undertake the development of the project. This lead to the Spartan Cruiser of which sixteen examples were built.

Percival had designed a remarkable three-seat touring monoplane which he had named the Gull. It was to achieve worldwide fame. Although the design had been offered to a number of well established aircraft manufacturers, all were strongly opposed to such a design, therefore Percival had no option, if the aircraft was to be built, but to do it himself! In collaboration with Lt Cdr E. B. W. Leake who undertook the financial arrangements, the

The wing structure of the only known remaining D1 Series Gull during its restoration by J. F. Neefs. It is now exhibited in the Brussels Air Museum (J. F. Neefs).

prototype was constructed by the Lowe-Wylde British Aircraft Company at their works in Maidstone and the machine was entered in the Kings Cup Air Race of 1932.

As only the prototype existed it was, of necessity, flown extensively for demonstration and test purposes. On one of these flights a forced landing was necessary, supposedly in Scotland, during which the wing was extensively damaged. The machine was returned to Brooklands for repair where, as constructional drawings were not available, the wings of the Hendy 302(G-AAVT) were stripped down and used as a pattern to enable the wings of the Gull to be rebuilt in time for the Kings Cup.

Although during the race the Gull only gained twelfth place (the winner being W. L. Hope flying a Fox Moth), it created a sensation by covering the 1,200 mile course as a perfectly standard touring aircraft and at an average speed of 142 mph. Throughout the race the machine behaved perfectly although for a brief moment Captain Percival had cause for concern when the exhaust pipe burned through.

In the 1930s, a gentleman by the name of Everling had devised a formula using various parameters such as wing area, power available, airscrew efficiency etc. by which the performance of an aeroplane could be calculated and the resulting figure, known as the Everling Factor, could be directly compared with the all-round efficiency figure using the same formula for other aircraft. It was found, by using this, that the overall efficiency of the Gull was even higher than that of the Schneider Trophy Aircraft. For weeks the pros and cons over the findings raged in the correspondence columns of the aviation journals. Whatever the outcome, the Gull became a most desirable machine, so, encouraged by the favourable reception, arrangements were made to market it, fully equipped, for the sum of £1,250. The

The original undercarriage units of the Gull had four compression springs, single attachment points and were strut-braced (J. F. Neefs).

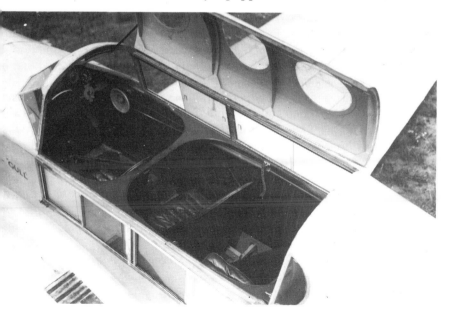

This photograph of the prototype Gull G-ABUR shows the seating arrangement with the transverse strut at the back of the pilot. The tail trimming wheel is on the starboard wall of the cabin (Flight).

operation was managed by Captain Percival from his home at 81, S George's Square, London and the construction of the production aircraf was contracted to George Parnall & Sons at their works in Yate, Gloucestershire.

Allocated the design letter 'D', the Gull was the first low-wing cantilever monoplane to be put into production in the British Empire. It was conventional in its construction, the primary fuselage being a plywood box, rectangular in cross-section, reinforced with spruce longerons and frames capped by a tertiary coaming of ply supported by laminated spruce frames. The coaming was extended over the cabin area by glazed panels and to allow access, the port side-panel was hinged at the bottom with the roof light hinged on the fixed starboard panel to enable it to be raised to give the necessary head clearance. Both side-panels were fitted with large sliding windows. On the prototype, the roof-panel was fitted with three circular transparent lights but these were soon replaced by a fully glazed unit.

A windscreen of five flat glass panels sloped down to a ply coaming over the instrument panel to complete the fuselage structure. All external plywood surfaces were protected by a covering of Madapolam doped on to the surfaces. The bottom longerons were stepped to receive the box-spar of the cantilever wing which was built in three sections.

The centre-section was of constant chord and thickness while the outer panels tapered in both chord and thickness. The Henderson method of construction was used in which two spruce members and ply spars of equal depth were braced by a lattice of spruce members which took the tortional and drag loads. Ribs of spruce and ply were attached to this assembly and the leading-edge was covered with ply to preserve aerodynamic efficiency. A section of the outer-panels aft of the rear spar and extending to the high aspect ailerons could be unlocked and raised to give the necessary clearance when the wings were folded. Hinge-pins for this purpose were incorporated in the rear spar joint plates.

At the front spar the joint-pins could be easily withdrawn and were fitted with an ingenious interlocking system which prevented the insertion of the top pin until the bottom one was fully home. The gap between the centre-section and the outer-panel was covered by a quickly detachable

fairing strip which, as a secondary precaution, could only be fitted when both pins were in situ.

The empennage units were also cantilever structures, the fin and tailplane employing two spars, the rudder and the elevator one. The single unit tailplane was pivoted at the front spar with a cable-operated screw-jack at the rear spar to adjust the angle of incidence in flight for trim.

The hydraulically-damped wheel units of the undercarriage were attached by single bolts to fittings at the extremities of the front spar of the centre-section and were strut-braced to take the landing loads. The fabricated wheel fork (which had four compression springs), the wheel with its Palmer low-pressure tyre and the Bendix hydraulic brake were enclosed by a semi-detachable streamlined fairing. Bolted to the sternpost was a sprung tail-skid which orientated.

Initially an inverted four-cylinder air-cooled Cirrus Hermes IV engine driving a Fairey fixed-pitch metal airscrew provided the power and was mounted on a triangulated structure of tubular steel bearers which were bolted to fittings on the longerons at the front of the fuselage. A bulkhead of aluminium and asbestos was screwed to the front bulkhead of the fuselage to provide fire protection. The side panels of the engine cowlings were hinged to a fixed top cowling for easy access and were secured by Dzus fasteners to a fixed bottom tray. The cowlings were completed by a fixed nose cowling which incorporated a large aperture through which the air was ducted to cool the cylinders.

Fuel was drawn from two 20 gallon tanks located between the spars of the outer wing via a selector cock mounted on the spar-box within the cabin

The prototype Percival Gull created such a good reception that it was marketed by Capt E. W. Percival and Lt Cdr E. B. W. Leake, fully equipped, for the price of £1,250.

17

The 22nd Gull G-ACPA, originally owned by Lt Cdr Leake, was converted to incorporate the front-hinged cabin doors of the later products and a tail wheel in place of the original skid as seen in this photograph. It was the last Gull to be built by Geo. Parnell and Sons (Hunting Percival Aircraft Ltd).

and dual engine-driven pumps. Mounted in the leading-edge of the centre-section on the port side was a three gallon surface cooled oil tank. All tanks were fitted with visual sight gauges and were clearly visible from the pilot's seat.

The cabin, situated above the wing, accommodated a pilot at the front and slightly to the port side with a compression strut at his back and between the top longerons. Two passengers were carried in staggered seats behind him, an arrangement which provided ample leg room; the middle occupant sitting with his feet in a well between the spars. A trimming wheel was located on the starboard wall of the fuselage with the engine control levers on the left and to reduce the noise level, all the walls were covered with padded leather and the floor with high grade carpet.

The prototype, allocated the registration G-ABUR, had an all-up weight of 2,050 lb (1,170 lb empty), was 24 ft 8 in long with a wing span of 36 ft which could be reduced to 12 ft 10 in by folding the outer wings. When fitted with the Cirrus Hermes engine, the Gull cruised at 125 mph and had a maximum speed of 145 mph over a range of 700 miles. Alternative engines could be fitted; the de Havilland Gipsy Major being offered as a direct replacement and the more powerful 160 hp six-cylinder Napier Javelin. With the latter the cruising speed increased to 140 mph and the maximum speed raised to 160 mph. G-ABUR served as a trials and flight-test vehicle for the alternative engine installations and gave yeoman service all over Europe until 1935 when it was written-off in Northern Rhodesia during an attempt by Man Mohan Singh to establish a new Cape record.

As interest grew in the Gull it became obvious that operations needed to be placed on a firmer footing so, in 1933, the Percival Aircraft Company was floated by Capt Percival and Lt Cdr Leake with Percival as the Managing Director and Chief Designer. For the six years he retained this post he was the driving force behind the Company. A Head Office and Drawing Office was established at 20, Grosvenor Square, London; the latter being under the control of R. H. Bound.

For two years construction had been sub-contracted and during that time 24 Gulls had been built by George Parnall & Sons but, by 1934, the demand had reached such a level as to warrant the establishment of a production facility. This was located at Gravesend with W. A. Summers appointed as Works Manager. At about the same time A. A. Bage was appointed to the post of Chief Draughtsman and became instrumental in converting the basic designs of Percival into the graceful and practical machines for which the Company was to become renowned.

During the production of the first twenty-four aircraft, many refinements had been incorporated. The rake of the windscreen had been increased, the cabin roof fully glazed and the horn-balance removed from the rudder. An air-brake had been fitted on the bottom of the fuselage immediately aft of the engine cowlings. But with the establishment of a

Jack Lavender, the Service Manager, prepares to start the Gull G-ADPR used by Jean Batten on her record-breaking flights (Flight).

production facility, major design changes were now possible!

On the original concept, due to the high sides of the fuselage, access to the cabin was not good. To overcome this the fuselage was re-designed and the top longerons were lowered over the cabin area. At the same time, the compression strut between the longerons was removed thus freeing the cabin from all obstructions. As a further improvement, large spring-balanced doors on both sides replaced the hinged side and roof panels and a luggage compartment, accessible through a hinged door on the port side, was provided aft of the cabin above the top longerons.

The undercarriage was also re-designed to incorporate a cast wheel fork attached to a single hydraulically-damped compression leg, splined to prevent rotation, rigidly mounted in brackets on the front spar. The compression leg was braced by small struts in the longitudinal and lateral planes to dissipate the landing loads. The removal of the compression springs from the wheel forks allowed the undercarriage fairings to be reduced in size and the re-location of the bracing struts enabled them to be completely removable. At the stern, a fully castoring and self-centring tail-wheel replaced the former skid.

Although three engines, the Cirrus Hermes IV, the Napier Javelin III and the de Havilland Gipsy Major could be fitted as alternative power units, it was decided to offer the de Havilland Gipsy Six of 200 hp as a further option. When fitted with this unit the performance of the Gull was again enhanced. The cruising speed increased to 152 mph while the maximum speed was raised to 166 mph.

By 1935 the Gull had been developed into its final form. The number of panels in the windscreen had been reduced from five to four and the rather ineffective air-brake beneath the fuselage has been replaced by more efficient split trailing edge flaps operated by an ingeniously designed mechanism that eliminated all aerodynamic loads. A further feature of the mechanism was that the position of the operating lever indicated the amount of flap depression.

The undercarriage had also received a final aerodynamic clean-up and the re-designing of the attachment brackets reduced the 6 ft 9 in track to 6 ft 5½ in. With these modifications and the careful attention given to the finish, (Percival was always pedantic about this) the performance increased still further. With the de Havilland Gipsy Six the cruising speed was pushed up to 155 mph and the top speed to 178 mph an increase of some 12 mph. During its development the all-up weight of the Gull had increased from 2,050 lb to 2,300 lb (2,450 lb for the Gull Six).

A livery of silver wings, tailplane and elevator with turquoise fuselage, fin and rudder, undercarriage fairings and engine cowlings was the standard finish but, at extra cost, customers could stipulate the livery and, indeed, any airframe modification they wished. An example of the lengths the Company would go to satisfy these requirements is well illustrated by the special Gull built for the Maharajah of Jodphur! In this, the standard three-seat cabin layout was extensively modified, in fact virtually re-

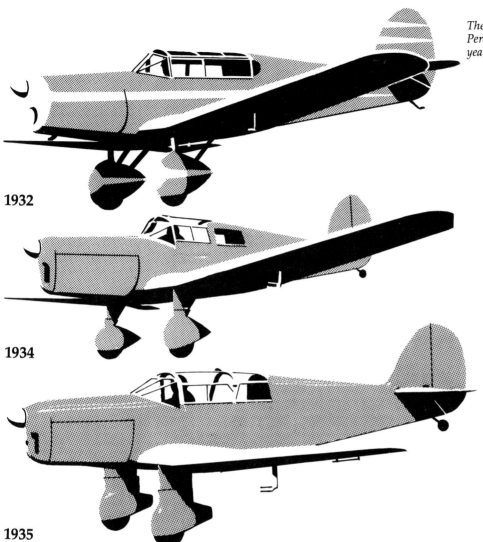

The changing shape of the Percival Gull over its four year production period.

1932

1934

1935

designed, to become a tandem two-seat aircraft with dual controls and open cockpits! Only one version was built and carried the registration VT-AGV.

Because of its performance the Gull became, almost, the standard mount for record seeking aviators who did much to promote aeroplanes as a fast and reliable form of transport. The pattern was set in 1933 by that well known Australian aviator (Sir) Charles Kingsford Smith who established a new England to Australia record flying a Gull which he had named 'Miss Southern Cross' and carried the registration G-ACJV, later changed to VH-CKS. He landed at Darwin on the 10 December 7 days 4 hr 50 min after taking off from Lympne. His Gull was the nineteenth to be built.

Percival continued the pattern in 1934 by flying the 640 miles between Gravesend and Copenhagen in four hours at an average speed of 160 mph and in June of the following year (1935) became the first aviator to fly to

Africa and back in one day by flying G-ADEP to Oran and back, completing the round journey in 14 hr 30 min. These feats, in addition to gaining the Company much needed publicity, were considered to be outstanding performances of navigation for which Percival was awarded the Johnston Trophy and the Oswald Watt Gold Medal.

Having been proved a reliable machine which was capable of maintaining high speeds over considerable distances, the Gull was soon establishing new records. In November 1935, H. F. Broadbent left Croydon on a ferrying flight in VH-UVA for (Sir) P. Gordon Taylor. He arrived in Australia 6 days 21 hr 19 min after leaving England and in doing so broke the record established by Kingsford Smith in 1933. In the same month Jean Batten flew G-ADPR from England to Brazil in 2 days 13 hr crossing the 2,000 miles of the South Atlantic in 13 hr 15 min which in itself was a record performance. For this outstanding flight she was awarded the Britannia Trophy.

Further outstanding flights were made in 1936. In May, Amy Mollison (née Johnson) established a new England to Cape Town record in G-ADZO which was the last Gull to be registered in the United Kingdom. Her outward journey took 3 days 6 hr 25 min and the return flight 4 days 16 hr 18 min. The first-ever flight from England to New Zealand was made by Jean Batten. She left Lympne on the 5 October and reached her native land 11 days 1 hr 25 min later; in doing so she established a new England to Australia record beating that set by Broadbent in the previous year by the handsome margin of 24 hours. On 26 October a fellow New Zealander, L. Erle Clark, flew the same route in G-ACUL, a Gull IV – Jean Batten's machine was the more powerful Gull VI – and reached Wigram on the 15 November, having been airborne for 12 hours over the Tasman Sea.

In May of the following year (1937) H. L. Brook flying the Gull VI previously used by Amy Mollison for her record flights, G-ADZO, made a record dash from Cape Town to England, arriving at Heston in 4 days 18 min and in October Jean Batten added yet another record to her already impressive collection by flying from Australia to England in 15 days 18 hr 15 min. Although otherwise standard aircraft, to enable the Gulls to fly the exceptionally long distances needed to establish these records, in addition to the optional fuel tanks which were fitted in the centre-section between the spars, a long-range tank was installed in the rear of the cabin normally occupied by the passengers.

From 1932 until production was terminated in 1936, a total of 47 Gulls were built of which 29 were of the D1 and D2 Series, the latter being of the Gull IV type. The remaining 19 were of the D3 Series – the Gull VI – and included the only open two-seat version to have been constructed. Three of the D2 Series Gull IV machines, D42 G-ACXY (Gipsy Major), D44 G-ACPA (Javelin III) and D45 G-ACUL (Gipsy Major) were converted to the D3 standard by fitting them with the de Havilland Gipsy Six engine.

During the Second World War Jean Batten's Gull VI, G-ADPR, was impressed into the Royal Air Force as AX866 and used for communication duties. While with the RAF it was fitted with an undercarriage from a Proctor and certain modifications applicable to the Proctor aircraft only were incorporated. In 1946 it was repurchased by Percival Aircraft Ltd, by then a member of the Hunting Group of Companies, and was frequently the star attraction at numerous air shows. It was then completely re-furbished and presented for safe-keeping to the Shuttleworth Collection and was ferried to Old Walden on 25 April 1961 shortly before Hunting Aircraft, as it had become, was absorbed into the (then) British Aircraft Corporation.

The only Gull of the D1 Series known to exist was discovered in 1979 in Belgium. It was D29, the ninth machine to be built, originally registered to Sir Philip Sassoon on 12 March 1933 and based at Lympne. In June of 1934 the registration was transferred to Sir John Kirwan and based at Heston but in December of the same year was written-off in a crash. The remains were acquired by a Belgian and were stored in a garage where they remained until the building was about to be demolished.

When the aircraft was discovered it was in an appalling state. The wings had been sawn off and many parts, including the Napier Javelin III engine, one of the undercarriage legs and all the fairings had long-since disappeared. Rain pouring through the roof had played havoc with the structure. Nevertheless when the, literally, heap of junk was offered to the Brussels Air Museum it was readily accepted, where, in the hands of J. F. Neefs and others, G-ACGR has been painstakingly restored.

A greater proportion of the Gull production was destined for the 'home market' although a great many, when they were offered for sale on the second-hand market, found ready buyers in all corners fo the world. The prototype carried the construction number D20 (for some reason known only to himself, Percival always chose to start his production numbers at 20)

A unique Gull, the only open version, constructed for the Maharajah of Jodphur. Carrying the registration VT-AGV it was destroyed in a crash in 1938.

and, as previously stated, the registration G-ABUR. It was used as demonstration and development vehicle until it was 'written-off' by Man Mohan Singh during his attempt on the Cape record in 1935. During its life the machine was fitted with a variety of power units and in 1933, when fitted with the Napier Javelin III engine of 160 hp had a performance superior to the fighter aircraft of that period.

The second machine, D21, enjoyed an active life of under one year. It was first owned by W. Lindsay Everard MP and was registered to him on 10 November 1932 as G-ACAL and named 'Leicestershire Fox'. He had the machine for a short time only for, in the early part of 1933, the Gull, a D2 Series aircraft fitted with a Javelin III engine, was transferred to the British Air Navigation Company who used it for fast newspaper work. After a few months service, when returning from an assignment in France in foul weather on 1 October, crashed at Sandhurst killing the company's chief pilot, A. J. Styran and I. C. MacGilchrist who was the company's manager. The third machine (D22) fared much better! This was, on the 24 March 1933, registered as G-ABUV powered by a Hermes IV engine, to C. S. Napier who kept it for six months. It was then acquired by Surrey Flying Services Ltd who operated it on charter and photographic work from August 1933 until October 1935 when it was transferred to M. Maxwell, also of Croydon. Almost a year later it was no more, for, after four years and nine months since first leaving the factory, it was destroyed on 2 November 1936 at Nice in France.

The next two Gulls, D23 (G-ACFJ) and D24 (G-ACAT) were both initially registered to Captain Percival, the former, powered by a Gipsy Major, being in his possession from 8 April 1933 until it passed to Guy de Chateabrun, Percival's agent in France, in January 1936 when it was re-registered F-AOZS. The other, G-ACAT, remained with Percival for a short period only after it was registered to him on 20 March 1933 as it was sold to an Australian in the April of the same year and re-registered VH-UQW. This machine was fitted with a Hermes IV engine.

D25, fitted with a Gipsy Major engine, was registered on 8 April 1933 to the British Air Navigation Company of Heston and carried the registration G-ACGC. It was, as was the ill-fated G-ACAL, used on newspaper work until it was sold, in January 1935, to Flt Lt N. C. Forbes and based at Netheravon until sold to Brazil where it carried the registration PP-BAA. G-ACFY (D26) was also first registered to Captain Percival on 8 April 1933 until it was sold to A. V. Roe and Company who used the aeroplane on communication duties from January 1935 until it was transferred to A. Collinge in June 1936. The aircraft was based at Woodford throughout this period until it was sold abroad a year later.

Loel Guinness purchased D27 and, equipped with a Gipsy Major engine, was based at Heston from 8 May 1933 with the registration G-ACLG. In November of 1934 it was acquired by Indian National Airways Ltd where it flew as VT-AVF and D28 was to exist for thirteen years before being scrapped at Thame in 1946. This aeroplane was first owned by A. V. M. E.

A. Borton and remained in his hands from 11 May 1933 until sold to C.T.F. Aviation Ltd of Thame in June 1940. Whether it flew during the years of hostilities is not known, but it remained in their hands until January 1946 when it passed to F. C. Bettison. It must have been in a very sorry state as it was soon scrapped. D29 (G-ACGR) fared much better and, as reported earlier in this chapter, is now preserved in the Brussels Air Museum, albeit in a non-airworthy condition, as one of the earliest examples existing of this remarkable aircraft.

As so frequently happened, the first registration of G-ACHA (D30) was to E. W. Percival. This was on 17 June 1933 but a couple of months later, in August, it was purchased by Airwork Ltd of Barton who used it for two years, until December when it was exported to Australia as VH-UTF. Although originally fitted with a Napier Javelin III engine it was converted to the D2 standard by installing a de Havilland Gipsy Six. D31 was also exported, this time to France, three years after it had been first registered to I. C. MacGilchrist on 24 May 1933. Before going to France in May 1936 it was in the hands of Brian Allen Aviation Ltd and the British Air Navigation Company who used it to cover the Italian-Abyssinian war of 1935.

The Gipsy Major powered G-ACHT (D32) was also owned by the Company from the 14 June 1933 until July 1936 flying from Gravesend and Luton until it left these shores in December of the same year.

After two years with Mrs A. Cleaver – it was registered to her on 20 July 1933 as G-ACIP – D33 was purchased by H. M. Schmitt of Holland and given the registration PH-HCA and D34, when in the hands of Henly's Ltd, suffered a most unfortunate demise when during take-off on 20 February 1935, one year and four months after first being registered to W. G. Robinson on 26 October 1933 as G-ACIR, it crashed and burst into flames.

After achieving an average speed of 143.97 mph in the 1935 Kings Cup, the Gipsy Major powered Gull VH-UVH was flown to Australia but on arrival at Goulburn in New South Wales on the 3 December 1935 was totally destroyed in a crash (Fox).

The instrument panel of the Gull mounting from left to right and top to bottom the rev counter, air speed indicator, altimeter, oil temperature, oil pressure, turn and bank, inclinometer, fuel contents and below it the clock. The magneto switches are at the bottom left-hand corner.

At the same time as G-ACLG joined Indian National Airways Ltd, so did D35 (G-ACIS) carrying the registration VT-AFU, and seven months later these two Gulls were joined by a third. This was G-ACLJ (D40) and it joined the fleet as VT-AGO in June 1935. G-ACIS was first registered on the 25 July 1933 to Air Service Training Ltd and G-ACLJ to Percival Aircraft Ltd on 18 November 1933, remaining in their hands until passing to Henly's Ltd in March 1934. D34 was also a stock aircraft being registered to the Company as G-ACPJ on 1 November 1933 before going to Japan as J-BASC in March of the following year.

The Gipsy Major powered D37 came to a watery end when it crashed in the English Channel on 2 May 1934 six months after being registered to N. M. Gazdar. Parts of G-AJCR were washed ashore at Berck thirteen days later.

Both D38 and D39 were exported to Australia after first appearing on the British Register; D38 as G-ACJW to Lt P. Randolph of Sherborne, Dorset on 18 September 1933 and D39 as G-ACJV to (Sir) Charles Kingsford-Smith whose exploits have already been noted. G-ACJW left the British Isles to become VH-UTC in November 1934 and served its Australian owners well before being withdrawn from use in January 1946.

The histories of D41, 43, 63 and 66 have yet to be traced, but D42 carrying the registration G-ACXY was used by Percival Aircraft Ltd from 22 October 1934 until going to France in February 1936. During its service with the Company it was re-engined with a de-Havilland Gipsy Six. G-ACPA (D44) was likewise converted. The first owner of this machine was Lt Cdr E. W. B. Leake who was the co-founder of the Company. He had the Gull from 16 April 1934 until February 1935 when it passed into the ownership of S. L. Turner, apparently for six months, as in August it was registered to Brian Allen Aviation Ltd. After serving with that Company for two months G-ACPA crashed at Avignon, France, on the 2 October 1935 en route to cover the Italian-Abyssinian War. This was the last Gull to be built under sub-contract by George Parnall and Sons; henceforth all production was undertaken by Percival Aircraft Ltd at their works in Gravesend.

The advantage of a production facility under the direct control of the Company was reflected in D45, the twenty fifth Gull to be built and the first machine to benefit from the undoubted skill of Arthur Bage, who did so much to develop the basic designs of E. W. Percival into the graceful and efficient aeroplanes for which the company became renowned. With its redesigned fuselage and undercarriage, G-ACUL was first registered to Lt P. Randolph who had disposed of 'CJW' in favour of the more powerful Gipsy Six engined version. Two years later, during October and November, it was flown to New Zealand and remained there as VK-AES. This modification was incorporated retrospectively in D30 (G-ACPA), D42 ('CXY) and D44 ('CPA).

The first owner of D46 was Miss Diana Williams being registered to her as G-ACUP on 7 July 1934. Almost three years later it was in the possession of S. K. Davies although still based at Cardiff. Just before the war, in June 1939, it was flown out to Australia where it was re-registered VH-ACM. Ten years later, in April 1949, the Gull was restored to an airworthy condition and again re-registered, this time as VH-CCM. Some sixteen years later this veteran, then thirty-four years old, showed that she was still capable of giving other competitors a run for their money by winning the Warana Air Race held at Archerfield, Brizbane, on 6 October 1968.

On 29 October 1934 D47, four days after being registered as G-ACYS, left Croydon in the care of A. F. Muir on a delivery flight to India for its owner, the Maharajah of Patiala. It was then registered VT-AGY and, as far as can be established, remained with him until impressed in March 1942, and given the serial HX794. Both D48 and D49 were first owned by Percival Aircraft, the latter being registered as G-ADEP on 20 March 1935 and the former as G-ADUE six days later. Both aircraft served as demonstrators; 'DUE until February 1938 when, as F-AQNA, it passed to the Marquis d'Aulan and eventually to Monsieur de Suares of Remes; 'DEP until January 1936 when it was acquired by Brian Allen Aviation Ltd who found an overseas buyer for it in August. While owned by the Company, G-ADEP was used by Captain Percival for his dash to Africa and back in one day, the feat for which he was awarded the Johnston Trophy and the Oswald Watt Gold Medal.

The next Gull, D50, was registered as G-ADFA on the 17 April 1935 for Charles E. Gardner the well known competition pilot of that era who flew it

Series D3 Gull HB-OFU, the 45th machine to be built, was registered to Ariane Dufaux in 1937. It returned to the United Kingdom 40 years later and was given the registration G-AERD.

in, and won, the Siddeley Trophy Air Race of 1935 at an average speed of 170.08 mph. A year later it was in the hands of R. Ince until it passed to Vickers Armstrong Ltd of Weybridge and used as a company hack. It was finally scrapped in November 1945 after a life of ten years, somewhat different to that of ten days for D51. It crashed at Baden Baden in Germany on 6 June.

The Egyptian subsidiary of the Shell Oil Company purchased D52, it being registered to them as G-ADKX on 17 June 1935 and based at Almaza, Cairo. During the first year of service a comprehensive tour of Africa was undertaken in adverse conditions which, on return to base, necessitated an extensive overhaul by MISR Airlines.

A report submitted by that company on 30 May 1936 painted a horrific picture of an aircraft held together by faith, hope and charity. A considerable proportion of the fuselage skin was in need of replacement, the longerons had become detached at the stern-post and the roof had badly distorted causing gaps around the doors. The starboard front spar of the centre section required rebuilding and many of the gussets were in need of regluing. In addition, the skin of the trailing-edge flaps had deteriorated to such an extent that its replacement was recommended and the wing panels which allowed the wings to be folded were badly warped – but how this was to be rectified was not stated.

Nevertheless, the repairs were successfully completed and 'DKX continued to fly with Shell Oil until October 1940 when Lt Col N. A. Blandford-Newson became the proud owner – but only for one month as in November the civilian livery was changed to drab camouflage and the serial number AX698.

G-ADOE (D53) began her twelve year life with the North Sea Aerial & General Transport Co of Brough staying with them for just over a year before being purchased by Blackburn Aircraft Ltd in December 1936 and used throughout the war as a company hack until March 1945 when it was procured by Air Couriers Ltd of Heston and the original Cirrus Major was replaced by a Gipsy Major. In June 1947 'DOE had a new owner, G. Chappelle-Knight of Jersey, but four months later, on 7 October, the Gull was ditched in the English Channel just off Ferring in Sussex.

Hooton was the base for D54 from 19 August 1935 until August of the following year when the original owner, W. R. Porter, sold it to M. Lejeune Esby of France; the registration being changed from G-ADMI to F-APEI. D55 was to become the most famous of all the Gulls built. It was first registered as G-ADPR on 12 September 1935 to Jean Batten and used by her, as narrated earlier in this chapter, on all but a few of her epoch making flights.

Although D55 was probably the most famous of all the Gulls, D56 was most certainly the most unique being the only two seat Gull with open cockpit to be built. It was registered to its owner, the Maharajah of Jodphur, as VT-AGV and ferried out to India by A. F. Muir. In 1938 it was severely damaged in a crash and the remains were transported to Luton where it was hoped that the machine would be rebuilt but, unfortunately, this was not to be. During the Kings Cup Air Race flown on 6 and 7 of September 1935 C. J. Melrose achieved an average speed of 143.97 mph in the Gipsy Major powered Gull (D57) carrying the registration VH-UVH. On 2 November he left Croydon on a flight to Australia but on arrival at Goulburn, New South Wales on the 3 December 'UVH crashed and was totally destroyed.

If D55 was the most famous and D56 was the most unique then D58 must go down in history as being owned by the most eccentric of aviators – Alice, the Duchess of Bedford. She became known as 'the flying grandmother' who began flying by taking lessons in 1928 and making her first solo from Lewsey Farm, between Luton and Dunstable, on 8 April 1930 at the ripe old age of 69 years. When she purchased her Gull, G-ADSG, on 3 October 1935 she was 75 years of age and already owned other aircraft. After she had disappeared in mysterious circumstances on what should have been a routine flight from the private air strip at Woburn to Girton and back, all the aeroplanes owned by her were bequeathed to her pilot, Flt Lt Raphael Chevallier and in December the Gull was disposed of to R. C. Preston of Newtownards. The next owner was W. Fairweather of Muzzaffarpur and it went to India in April 1939 with a new registration VT-ALT. During the war it was impressed for service use as MA927.

D59 was also impressed into the Royal Air Force in August of 1940 as BD 165 but in the same month (it is believed) was destroyed by enemy bombing before actually entering service. It was first registered to the Asiatic Petroleum Company on 21 October 1935 as G-ADSM and used by them until flown to Ford and the unfortunate end. The exploits of VH-UVA (D60) in the hands of H. F. Broadbent have been chronicled earlier and D61 was never registered. It was completed, using various unserviceable components, as a full-size model, sans engine and interior fitments, and used as an exhibit at various Air Shows.

D63 was the last Gull to appear, pre-war, on the British Register. It was G-ADZO and registered to Percival Aircraft Ltd on 17 December 1935. After a year with the Company it went to H. L. Brook of Sherburn-in-Elmet but after the expiry of the C of A on 8 February 1938 was scrapped. All that is known of D64 is that it was exported to South Africa as ZS-AHD.

On 8 July 1984 the port wing of D65 was badly damaged when it crashed, during take-off, into a taxying Piper Cheroke – fortunately without fatalities. First registered as HB-OFU, this aircraft was sold to Ariane Dufaux of Geneva. It left Heston on 19 January 1937 on its delivery flight, arriving at Cointreau, Geneva, Switzerland on the following day after an overnight stop at Le Touquet, France. It was flown regularly before the war on trips to France but came to grief in June 1942. It was not until August 1946 that repairs were completed and the Gull had a new owner, Alfredo Habib. After a further Swiss owner, J. Augsburger, it returned to England and the skilled hands of Cliff Lovell and the contemporary registration G-AERD on 16 September 1977. It was given a thorough overhaul prior to its appearance at many Air Shows. Disaster struck at Thruxton in Hampshire on 30 May 1981 when a precursor of the 1984 crash occurred. The port wing dropped on take-off!

The resulting impact severely damaged all parts of the aircraft but after extensive and painstaking repairs 'ERD was restored to her former glory and flying again in March 1983 with a resplendent livery of silver and red. Soon after it was purchased by Neil Jensen who based the Gull at Redhill until its final accident at Cranfield on 8 July 1984.

The Shell Oil Company of South Africa were the owners of the last Gull to be built. It was registered to them as ZS-AKI and delivered on 18 October 1937, remaining in their possession until it was impressed into the South African Air Force as 1430 during 1940.

CHAPTER 2
THE VEGA GULL

Although the sales of the Gull had been good – in those days it was not necessary to build and sell hundreds to break even – it seemed prudent to produce a four seat version, so, early in 1935, work started on such an aircraft under the design letter 'K'. It was to become the Vega Gull, the prototype being first flown by Capt Percival from Gravesend in November of the same year.

Basically the same aerodynamic configuration of the Gull was retained and to achieve approximately the same wing loading of 13.67 lb/sq ft, the loading of the final version of the Gull VI, the area of the centre section was enlarged by 15 sq ft which gave a total wing area of 197 sq ft and resulted in a wing loading of 14.5 lb/sq ft. This modification increased the span to 39 ft 5 in, some seven feet greater than its predecessor, however the overall length was only six inches more. The aerodynamic balance was redressed by enlarging the empennage units, the tailplane and elevator being increased by a total of three square feet; the fin and rudder increasing proportionately.

The structural configurations of the Gull were also retained, the primary fuselage structure was still the well proven plywood box reinforced by longerons and frames with a tertiary coaming of ply supported on laminated spruce frames but, to accommodate four people in side-by-side seating, was increased by nine inches at its maximum width in the cabin area. The wing retained the Henderson method of construction, i.e. two spars of equal depth braced by a lattice of spruce members to take the torsional and drag loads, but to cater for the increased airframe and aerodynamic loads the entire structure was re-stressed.

With an all-up weight of 2,875 lb the Vega Gull was a much heavier aeroplane but a great deal of detail refinement had been undertaken. All the flying controls were enclosed within the structure (on the Gull the ailerons were operated by control levers and push-rods below the surface of the wing) and the undercarriage units were pure cantilever components braced in the fore-and-aft plane only by small compression struts to the rear spar which were enclosed within the fixed portion of the undercarriage fairings. The compression legs were originally the same as those fitted to the Gull with splines to retain alignment but this method was changed for the cheaper to manufacture 'knuckle-plates' which were just as effective.

The attention to detail paid off handsomely. The maximum speed of the Vega Gull was 173 mph which was only five miles an hour slower than the smaller and similarly powered Gull but, when fitted with the slightly more powerful de Havilland Gipsy Six Series II engine driving a variable pitch airscrew, the cruising speed increased to 158 mph, an improvement of two

The prototype Vega Gull seen here flying under the incorrect registration G-AEAD . . . it should have been G-AEAB. It was written-off in a crash near Lake Tanganyika on the 30 September 1936 while competing in the Schlesinger Air Race to Johannesburg.

miles an hour.

Initially the prototype aircraft (which, incidentally was priced at £1,550 and first flew with the incorrect registration G-AEAD – it should have been G-AEAB) was not fitted with dual controls and the trimming wheel was, as on the Gull, situated on the starboard wall of the cabin but this was soon moved to a more accessible position on the port side. When dual controls were eventually fitted a duplicate set of engine management levers was mounted on the centre line of the fuselage decking below the instrument panel.

In a review which appeared in 1 January issue of the *Aeroplane* for 1936 it was commented that the Vega Gull was practically as fast and landed as slowly, as the Gull and to return such a performance must, indeed, be efficient. This was substantiated during the Kings Cup Air Race flown on 10 and 11 July 1936.

Four Vega Gulls, the prototype G-AEAB (K20) flown by Misri Chand, G-AEKD (K28) owned and flown by Lt Patrick Randolph, G-AEKE (K29) owned by Sir Connop Guthrie and piloted by Charles Gardner and the 'Leicestershire Fox IV' registered G-AELE (K26) flown by P. Q. Reiss for the owner, W. Lindsay Everard, fought a private duel with the Miles team. The race was eventually won by Charles Gardner at an average speed of 164.47 mph on the final course of 312 miles.

To cover the 1,224 miles of the eliminating stage of the race, G-AEKE, the winning Vega Gull, has been fitted with the optional centre section tanks plus a long-range tank situated in the cabin. In preparation for the next important event in the aeronautical calendar, the Schlesinger Race to Johannesburg which was held in the October of 1936, the prototype was similarly equipped and both 'EAB and 'EKE were fitted with the slightly more powerful de Havilland Gipsy Six Series II engine driving a Hamilton variable pitch airscrew.

Conditions during the race which started from Portsmouth were far from ideal and gradually the field was reduced as aircraft and crews succumbed for one reason or another. The prototype, by then owned by D. W. Llewellyn, came to grief and was written-off on 30 September near Lake Tanganyika and only one aircraft completed the course. That was the Vega Gull G-AEKE crewed by C. W. A. Scott and the owner's son, Giles Guthrie. They landed at Rand Airport on 1 October having completed the gruelling race in 52 hr 56 min 56 sec to become the winners.

Abingdon, near Oxford, was the next venue for the start of a record-making flight when, on 4 September 1936 Mrs Beryl Markham took-off in VP-CKK, a Vega Gull (K34) bearing the name 'Messenger'. During the ensuing flight, strong headwinds were encountered which reduced the range and resulted in Mrs Markham landing short of her destination in Cape Bretton, Nova Scotia. During the emergency landing 'Messenger' ran into soft ground and sustained damage when it stood on its nose, but in spite of this, Mrs Markham gained the honour of being the first woman to make the crossing of the Atlantic from east to west in the record time of 21 hours.

The success of the Vega Gull in competitive flying continued in 1937 when, on 30 March, two Frenchmen, Mm. Passavy and Cornet, left Paris and 3 days 23 hr later landed in Saigon, in what is now Vietnam, and a further record was claimed by L. H. Brook when he completed a flight from Cape Town to England in 4 days 18 min. To complete the honours for that year, the Littorio Rally was won by Signor Parodi in competition with seventy-five aircraft representing nine countries. Apart from being converted to accommodate five people, his Vega Gull was a perfectly standard machine.

Although, in 1935, Harry Broadbent had established an England to Australia record, it had been taken away from him during the following year by Jean Batten. For those flights both aviators had used Gulls. In April 1938, Broadbent set out to re-capture the honours using the, by then, well established and proven Vega Gull and did so by a margin of 16 hr 58 min in the record time of 5 days 4 hr 21 min.

By 1938 a Series II version was in production, the first example being

Vega Gull G-AEKE was the only aircraft to complete the course in the Schlesinger Air Race. Crewed by C. W. A. Scott and Giles Guthrie it won the gruelling race, flying the course in 52 hrs 56 min 56 sec (Flight).

The Percival Vega Gull monoplane 'Messenger' being pushed out by Jack Lavender (at wing root) and some of his staff for a final check.

introduced on the thirty-ninth Vega Gull built (K59) which was registered G-AEYC. It differed from the original concept in as much that the windscreen was of moulded 'Perspex' – an early form of plastic – and the top lights in the rear of the cabin were deleted. Although the Vega Gull used by Broadbent (G-AFEH, K100) was a Series II machine, he found that the moulded windscreen caused too much distortion and had the former flat panels fitted.

During the production run from 1935 to 1939, a total of 90 Vega Gulls were constructed (including one rebuild) of which 30 were exported although a further 12 left these shores after first appearing on the British Register. A further 14 were purchased by the Air Ministry for use as communication aircraft, their numbers being augmented later as civil aircraft were impressed into the armed forces.

As recorded earlier in this chapter, the prototype, K20, was first registered to Percival Aircraft Ltd on 17 February 1936 and after serving as a demonstrator was sold to D. W. Llewellyn in September only to be destroyed on 30 September during the Schlesinger Air Race. The second machine, K21, was registered to the Hon. Drogo Montague as G-AECF on 30 March but a year later, in April 1937, was sold to France where it was registered F-AQCF and the third (K22) bearing the registration G-AEEM was initially built for Sir Charles Rose who retained it for a year before selling it to D. W. Llewellyn (who had previously owned the prototype) in January 1937. In November of the same year Bowmaker Ltd acquired the aircraft and based it at Luton until May 1939 when it was converted to Series II standard and exported to Sweden as SE-AHR only to be destroyed two years later after being shot down by a German fighter aircraft.

After being initially registered to Percival Aircraft as G-AEAS, K23 was sold to Vernon Motion in April 1936 but a few months later, in December, the registration was cancelled, no record being traced as to the reason for this. The next two aircraft were also exported after first appearing on the British Register – but this time they went to France; K24 to Percival's agent – Guy de Chateaubrun – in June 1937 as F-AQEA after first being registered to Percival Aircraft on 29 April 1936 as G-AEHA and K25 which was first registered to Col. A. Hamilton-Gaunt as G-AEIF on 12 May 1936 going to M. Roger Goldet as F-AQMZ in April 1938.

After an eventful start to its career when it participated in the gripping duel during the 1936 Kings Cup Air Race, K26 (G-AELE known as 'Leicestershire Fox IV') was lost when it was ditched in the Bay of Canche, near le Touquet, on 26 June 1939 and K27 was used extensively on commercial enterprises, first being registered to Commercial Air Hire Ltd on 31 May 1936. It passed to British American Air Services Ltd in September 1939 but in April of the following year was impressed as X9455 and served until October 1944 when it was scrapped.

G-AEKD (K28) and G-AEKE (K29) also featured in the noteable Kings Cup duel of 1936 and both were destroyed in crashes. The former, first registered to Lt Patrick Randolph (who had previously owned Gulls) on 13 June 1936 was destroyed in a crash, which also killed the owner, at Sanganer Aerodrome between Bombay and Jaipur, India, on 12 October 1937 and the latter, after being first registered to Sir Connop Guthrie on 7 June 1936 and winning the Kings Cup and Schlesinger Air Races was sold to Mrs Beryl Urquhart in October 1936. It crashed on 28 January 1938.

The Marquess of Douglas and Clydesdale was the first owner of K30 when it was registered to him as G-AELF in June 1936 but in the March of 1938 went to India as VT-AJZ. The next three Vega Gulls were eventually impressed into service use: K31 by the Royal Navy in March, 1940 as W9376 after first being registered to Sir George Lewis as G-AELS on 21 July 1936, K32 as X9349 (in March 1940) but was scrapped at Cardiff in December of the same year after a brief military service of nine months. It was originally in the service of the Anglo American Oil Company from 30 July 1936 as G-AELW. The last of the trio, K33, was first registered to G. W. Harben as G-AEMB on 24 August 1936 and based at Hatfield and impressed as X9371 in the March of 1940.

The Author happened to be around when the photographer took this picture on the prototype Vega Gull Series II (Aeroplane).

The exploits of K34, VP-KCC, used by Mrs Beryl Markham have already been narrated but little is known of the histories of the next seven machines apart from the fact that they were sold abroad. These and the other Vega Gulls sold to foreign owners are listed in the accompanying table.

The next Vega Gull for which records are available is G-AERH (K41) registered to W. R. Porter on 4 December 1936. While participating in the Isle of Man Race on 29 May 1937 it crashed into a house while taking-off from Hanworth and burst into flames. K42 was also destroyed in a crash when it spun in at Aboukir on 17 May 1941 where it was being used by the Station Flight after being impressed in the April of 1940 as X1033. Prior to this it was owned by Air Service Training Ltd being registered to them as G-AERL on 8 December 1936.

Both K45 and K46 were registered to Percivals as G-AEPS and 'ETD respectively, both registrations being made in the February of 1937. Later in the same month 'EPS was sold to P. G. Aldrich-Blake and just over a year later, in August 1938, was acquired by Airwork Ltd, Almaza, who sold it in October of the same year to Egypt where it was registered SU-AAX. 'ETD remained with the Company as a demonstration and general purpose aircraft until March 1939 when it passed to Barbara Chateaubrun. A year later this also went abroad, to Belgium, with the registration OO-ANC as did K47 a month earlier in February 1939. This Vega Gull was first registered as G-AETE to I. G. Williamson on 26 February 1937 and passed through the hands of W. H. Whitbread in September 1938 and Airwork Ltd of Heston two months later before being exported as OO-ANY.

Although, in effect, the de Havilland Aircraft Co Ltd of Hatfield was in competition with Percivals inasmuch that both companies were contenders in the same market, G-AEFT (K48) was purchased and used by them as a communications aircraft from 12 March 1937 until it was impressed into the Royal Navy in March 1940 as W9378 and based at Hatston. Its use by the Senior Service lasted for a mere six months as on 19 September it was extensively damaged when it skidded into a wall.

For a time, in addition to G-AETD, the Company operated four other Vega Gulls for demonstration purposes and charter. All were registered to the Company in 1937 the first being G-AEWO (K49) on 28 April. Two years later it was sold to MM. P. Pedroline and M. Vardi of Switzerland where it carried the registration HB-UTV. The second machine, first registered on 30 March, was destroyed in a crash at Johnstone near Renfrew on 3 July after a life of four months and the third, K59, the forerunner of the Series II aircraft, was registered as G-AEYC on 2 June. It was impressed in October 1939 and flew throughout the hostilities as W6464 until it was restored to the Civil Register in June 1946 in the ownership of Lambskin Exports Ltd. Based at Kidlington it flew for a further fourteen years before being severely damaged on 14 August 1960 thirty-three years after first being registered. The last of the quartette, G-AFAU (K69), first registered on 30 July was also impressed and served as X9332 from February 1940 until restored to the Civil Register as G-AIIT.

Both K52 and K57 were purchased by European Air Commerce Ltd to whom they were registered as G-AEWS and 'EXV respectively and based at Gatwick. The company flew them commercially until July 1938 when 'EWS were sold to C. H. Self. In the April of 1940 it was impressed into military use but, like so many of its sisters, had a very short service life. It crashed near Taunton in Devon on 10 October. G-AEXV was to fare much better. This aeroplane was impressed as X9391 in the March of 1940 and after six years of military service was restored to the Civil Register in December 1946 and flown by the Brevet Flying Club for a short time before being acquired by British & Continental Airways Ltd in the same month. After serving with them for four years it was finally dismantled at Southend in April 1950.

After being registered to W. L. Runciman, a noted sporting pilot of the time on 20 May 1937 as G-AEXU, K56 was also impressed and given the serial number X1032. In 1943 it was based at Aboukir. For a year G-AEYD (K60) was registered to the company before being sold to Cairns Aviation Ltd of Salisbury, Southern Rhodesia where it resided as VP-YBV and K65, after being owned by D. Schreiber as G-AEZJ from 15 July 1937, was sold a year later to T. J. Bendien of Almelo in Holland where it flew as PH-ATH.

All that is known of K66 and K67 (G-AEZK & G-AEZL respectively) is that they were owned by G. M. Tounge and F. C. J. Butler, both registrations being made in July 1937. They were 'called up' within a month of each other and served as X9339 and X9436. A little more is known of K70. This was registered to the Secretary of State for Air on 30 August 1937 as G-AFBO and used by the Attaché in Berlin as his personal aircraft. It was seized by the German authorities on the outbreak of war as was G-AFIM (K93) when it had to be abandoned at Le Bourget by its owner, Mrs H. M. Russell-Cooke, when France was overrun in May 1940.

Two further Vega Gulls were purchased by the Secretary of State for Air as personal aircraft for Air Attachés; K71, which first carried the serial number L7272 but appeared in the Civil Register as G-AFWG on 3 July 1939, was based at Buenos Aires and K109, the last Vega Gull to be built, took-off

A. R. Coleman of Norwich was the first owner of Vega Gull G-AFBC in 1937. Fifteen years later after serving throughout the war as X9340 it crashed at Eastleigh in Hampshire in July 1954 (Hunting Percival Aircraft Ltd).

This Vega Gull was flown by MM. Hirsch-Ollendorf in the Rallye Du Hoggar. It was placed 2nd in the general European classification. Note the French VP airscrew.

from Luton Airport on 27 July to be eventually based at Lisbon where it flew as G-AFVI (after first being allocated the serial P5992) until it crashed on 19 May 1944.

Eastleigh in Hampshire was the scene of the crash of G-AFBC (K75) on 12 July 1954, fifteen years after being first registered to A. R. Coleman of Norwich on 8 September 1937. From March 1940 it had served as X9340 until demobilised in the June of 1947 with A. J. Muir of Perth as the owner. It returned to Luton in July 1948 where it was operated by Anglo Continental Air Services Ltd until eventually sold to Lady Sherbourne. Its last owner was Grp Capt C. M. M. Grece. The collapse of the undercarriage on 1 February 1941 at Lydda resulted in the demise of K76 while serving as X1034. This Vega Gull, carrying the registration G-AFVA, started its career with Wrightson Air Hire Ltd of Heston on 27 August 1937. Almost two years later, in March 1939, E. Thomas became the owner and he based it at Ringway until it was impressed in May 1940.

1 June 1938 was a day on which gloom and despondency descended upon the staff of Percival Aircraft Ltd for it was on that day G-AFBR (K79), owned by the Indian Aviation Development Corporation of Bombay, crashed while in the circuit at Luton Airport prior to a visit to the Company. Although Mr Rushden, the Airport Manager, was at the scene of the crash with his ancient Crossley ambulance within minutes, there was little he could do as all the occupants had been killed on impact.

As a result of a demonstration at Martlesham Heath by Capt Percival before members of the Fleet Air Arm, the Royal Air Force and the Air Ministry, an order was placed which eventually lead to the supply of sixteen Vega Gulls for use as communications aircraft. This was quite a 'feather in

the cap' for Percival as the Air Ministry was not known to favour small manufacturers. As has been related previously, three of these, K70, K71 and K109 were earmarked as personal aircraft for various Air Attachés; the rest, covering K86 to K88, K94 to K97, K102, K103 and K105 to K108 being distributed amongst the Royal Navy and the Royal Air Force. One of the Navy's Vega Gulls, while being flown as an Admiral's barge, made a landing on an aircraft carrier without the use of arrester gear. The allocation of the serial numbers of these aircraft are given in the accompanying table.

To return to the histories of the remaining civil aeroplanes, G-AFBW (K82) was registered to R. E. Gardner of Hansey Green on 15 October 1937 and remained with him for two years before being sold to D. Stewart-Clarke of Macmerry in the June of 1939. It was impressed in January 1940 and served with the Royal Navy as W9377 based at Donibristle. Alex Henshaw,

L7272 was a Series I Vega Gull identified by the glazing above the rear cabin windows and the flat-panelled windscreen. This particular aeroplane was powered by a Gipsy Six engine driving a Fairey fixed pitch metal airscrew.

39

the maker of many records and winner of numerous air races was the first owner of K84, the aeroplane being registered to him as G-AFEA on 20 January 1938. During the war this Vega Gull was used by Gloster Aircraft Ltd of Hucclescote on communication duties until August 1946 when it was sold to Universal Flying Services Ltd. A year later it was in the hands of D. F. Little of Fairoaks who entered the fifteen-year-old veteran in the South Coast Air Race which started from Shoreham on 7 August 1951.

K89, 90 and 91 were all impressed, K89 as X9392 after being registered as G-AFEK on 18 February 1938 to R. D. Craig who sold it to the Earl of Amherst, K90 which was owned by R. E. Gardner (who had previously owned G-AFBW) from 21 July 1938 being registered to him as G-AFIT before entering the Services in September 1939 as W9375 and K91 which, as G-AFEM, belonged to Lt Col A. Hamilton-Gaunt before joining up as X9368. 'FEK was scrapped in 1944 and 'FEM in 1943.

G-AFGU (K92) existed for less than a month. After being registered to S. Smith of Woolsington on 23 April 1938 it crashed and burst into flames at Brundholme, Ghyll, Westmoreland, on the 14th of the following month. The fate of K93 (G-AFIM) has already been given and G-AFIE (K99) of Smith's Aircraft Instruments Ltd was based at Hatfield and destroyed by German bombs when at Hendon on 7 October 1940. H. F. Broadbent used K100, registered G-AFEH, on his record-breaking flight to Australia but it was sold to J. M. Barwick in January 1939. During the war it served as X9315 and was restored to the Civil Register in June 1946 being used by the Lancashire Aircraft Corporation of Squires Gate. After serving them for seven years it was scrapped at Squires Gate in April 1953.

After the war one of the Vega Gulls purchased off the production line by the Air Ministry, P5989 (K105), was acquired by Essex Aero Ltd and given the registration G-AHET on 9 July 1946. It remained with them for ten years after which it was sold to M. J. Taylor of Denham who kept it for just over a year passing it to Tourist Trophy Garage Ltd, Fairoaks, in August 1957. In the May of 1959 it was in the hands of E. N. Husbands of Fairwood Common but a year later, on 2 May 1960 it was damaged beyond repair in a forced landing near Liverpool.

Only one construction number, K104, remains unaccounted. It was used as a works construction number for the rebuilding of K68, F-AQIR!

Prior to 1940, only Jack Lavender the Service Manager was authorised to clear aeroplanes for flight. One morning a cantankerous Percival had crossed swords with him and, as usual, had resulted in Jack being fired. Completely un-ruffled, Lavender had promptly retired to the local hostelry for light refreshment before attending one of the local cinemas to view the latest offering from Hollywood.

During the afternoon Percival sent forth a decree that a Vega Gull should be made ready for demonstration to a potential customer. When told that it was not possible to meet his request Percival demanded to know the reason. 'Because you fired Lavender and he's the only person who can authorise the paperwork!' came the reply. 'Get the stupid bugger back!'

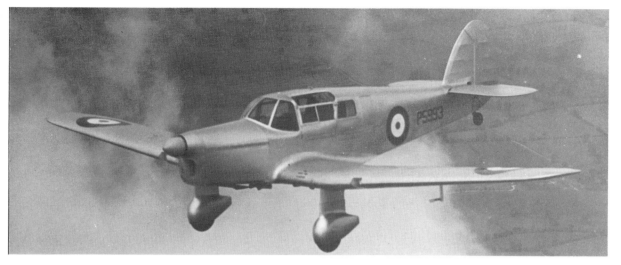

roared Percival, 'I don't care how, but get him back!'

Frantic telephone calls were made to all the local cinemas and a request that 'Would Jack Lavender please report to his company urgently.' was flashed up on all the screens. Jack ignored the appeals, sat back and enjoyed the film with greater relish! The following morning a contrite Percival apologised for his behaviour.

Series II Vega Gull P5993 was one of the last of the type to be constructed (Flight).

List of Vega Gulls purchased from the production line by foreign customers.

K34.	VP-KCC	K53.	F-APXA	K73.	VT-AIV
K35.	CF-BAR	K54.	Japan	K74.	VT-AIW
K36.	VH-UVG	K55.	VP-KCH	K77.	F-AQIG
K37.	F-APEX	K58.	VH-UZH	K78.	VT-AJQ
K38.	F-APIG	K61.	F-AQBV	K80.	VT-AJR
K39.	VP-KCD	K62.	VT-AIQ	K81.	F-AQEN
K40.	F-APIL	K63.	ZK-AFI	K83.	VH-ABS
K43.	F-APHX	K64.	HB-OMD	K85.	YI-CPF*
K44.	VP-KCE	K68.	F-AQIR	K86.	VH-ACA
K50.	F-APOL	K72.	VT-AJD	K101.	F-ARAU

Purchased by King Ghazi of Iraq.

List of Serial Numbers allocated to Vega Gulls purchased by the Air Ministry.

K33.	L7272 (G-AFWG)	K95.	P1751	K105.	P9598
K86.	P1749	K96.	P1752	K106.	P5990
K87.	P5986	K97.	P1753	K107.	P5993
K88.	P5987	K102.	P1754	K108.	P5991
K94.	P1750	K103.	P5988	K109.	P5992*

The last Vega Gull to be built.

The first three Q6 aircraft to be built. The prototype G-AEYE leads the flight with the second built, G-AFFD of Sir Philip Sassoon, on its right and the third built, YI-ROH for the King of Iraq, on its left (Flight).

CHAPTER 3

THE 'Q6'

By 1936 the publicity gained from the outstanding performances of the Gulls and Vega Gulls had done much to enhance the standing of the Company and initial design work had started on a twin-engined monoplane. The buildings at Gravesend were inadequate to meet the expanding demands but a new airport was under construction at Luton. This was within easy reach of London and the head office in Grosvenor Square and the space available was almost unlimited. A two-bay hangar had been built to accommodate the workshops and the design office had been located in the original Georgian farmhouse – hence the advertisement for a junior draughtsman to which I had replied.

After a brief introductory talk with Mr Bage, I was conducted to one of the small bedrooms and introduced to Mr Humpage and Mr Curtis to whom I was to supply draughting effort on the twin-engined monoplane which had been allocated the design letter 'Q'.

Frank Humpage was responsible for the fuselage design and Harold Curtis the engine installations. The engineering applied to aircraft was quite alien to the massive applications of hydraulics but under their kindly and expert tuition I quickly learned that 1 inch Whitworth bolts and 6 × 4 timbers were a thing of the past. I now had to think in terms of lightness combined with strength and how to calculate stresses. I found the work entirely different to that I had been doing and totally absorbing.

The 'Q' machine was, as previous products, of wooden construction. The primary fuselage structure from the front spar to the stern-post was a plywood box strengthened by frames and longerons. It was enclosed at the top by a tertiary coaming of ply supported on laminated spruce frames, the slab-sided appearance being relieved by supporting the Madapolam covering at the sides on light frames and stringers. A cantilever platform attached to the front frame of the fuselage box extended forward to carry the seats of the two crew members, the flying controls, the engine controls and the ancillary equipment. A fabric-covered nose structure of frames and stringers terminating in a spun aluminium nose cap completed the fuselage.

In addition to the two crew members, four passengers (five if the toilet was omitted) were accommodated in the comfortable cabin which was entered through a jettisonable door in the port side. Immediately opposite this was the toilet compartment and to the rear and accessible through a hatch was the luggage compartment. A circular emergency exit was provided in the roof of the cabin aft of the cockpit.

The stressed-skin mainplane, built in three sections, comprised two spars of spruce and ply, spruce and ply ribs and was, with the exception of

the ailerons, completely covered with a ply skin. The centre section was of constant chord and thickness and surface-cooled oil tanks of 3¾ gallon capacity, one for each engine, in the leading edge. The outer wing panels tapered in both chord and thickness and were attached to the centre section via steel plates bolted to the spars and pins. Four fuel tanks were mounted between the spars, two in the centre section and one in the root of each outer wing. This fuel capacity gave the aircraft a still air range of 700 miles.

Vacuum-operated split trailing-edge flaps extended from the fuselage to the high-aspect ailerons, their position being indicated by a rod which protruded through the upper surface of the wing. The large diameter operating ram – one for each flap – was mounted in the rear of each engine nacelle.

The two-spar tailplane was built as a single ply-covered unit and bolted directly to brackets mounted on the top longerons. The two-spar fin, fabric covered with a ply reinforced leading edge, was bolted directly to the sternpost. The rudder and elevator were both fabric covered and had single spars, ply ribs and trailing edges of oval aluminium tube. Both had trim-tabs which could be adjusted in flight by small crank-handles mounted on the control pedestal between and slightly forward of the crew seats.

The control column, mounted on the centre line of the aircraft, moved in the fore and aft plane only with a hinged section at the top carrying a half-wheel for the aileron control. This was normally canted to the left but when the machine was flown from the opposite seat it could be unlocked by withdrawing a self-locking pin and swung over. Movement was transferred to the aileron control cables by a system of chains and sprockets; a single

sprocket at the half-wheel moved, via a chain, a double sprocket at the hinge. A short chain around the second element of the double sprocket was connected to the aileron control cables.

Although it was envisaged that the aeroplane would be offered in two configurations, the 'Q4' and 'Q6', the former having de Havilland Gipsy Major engines of 120 hp, only the latter, fitted with the more powerful de Havilland Gipsy Six Series II engines driving de Havilland controllable-pitch airscrews, was built.

The underslung engines were mounted in triangulated bearers of steel tube (which also carried the undercarriage) bolted to the front and rear spars. Immediately behind the engine and bolted to the bearers was a fire-proof bulkhead of aluminium and asbestos sandwich.

Each undercarriage unit consisted of two legs, one on each side of the wheel, which incorporated steel springs in compression with hydraulic recoil dampers similar in design to those used on the Gull and Vega Gull. Each leg was pivoted on a heavy cross-tube incorporated in the engine mounting structure and braced by a radius tube attached to the lower end of each compression leg and the rear spar. When a retractable undercarriage was installed, the radius tubes were hinged at their centres; retraction being performed by a vacuum ram attached to the front spar and a cross-tube welded between the upper elements of the radius tubes. The undercarriage was locked in the 'down' position by the off-set hinges of the radius tubes and restrained by bungee cords. The undercarriage doors remained open when the undercarriage was lowered and were, in no way, connected by a linkage to the undercarriage unit. When these were retracted the doors were held in the closed position by bungee cords only. As the undercarriage was

The last aircraft to be built to the prototype standard was F-AQOK owned by Leon Sternberg de Armella. It returned to the UK and flew with Western Airways Ltd before being impressed as AX860 and based at Lee-on-Solent (Harold Cox).

45

With power on and everything down VH-ABY rumbles in to Luton Airport (Flight).

extended, guard tubes – or rather guide tubes – attached to the compression legs merely forced the doors open against the cords. Such a simple system with no form of positive locking would not be permitted on todays' metal masterpieces!

Although the 'Q' (it was never officially named the 'Petrel' – that was suggested by C. G. Grey who was at the time the Editor of the *Aeroplane*) was a six to seven seat aeroplane, its overall dimensions were not much greater than those of the Vega Gull. It had a wing span of 46 ft 8 in, a length of 32 ft 3 in, and an overall height of 9 ft 9 in. The loaded weight was 5,550 lb which gave a power loading of 13.4 lb/sq ft. The wing area of 278 sq ft gave a wing loading of 19.8 lb/sq ft. The maximum speed at sea level was 195 mph (206 mph with the undercarriage retracted) and cruised at 172 mph which increased to 181 mph when fitted with the optional retractable undercarriage. With the flaps lowered, the landing speed was 58 mph.

Although designed to have a retractable undercarriage, this was not fitted to the prototype, in fact four (although I can only recollect two) aircraft were fitted with this optional feature.

The prototype was first flown by Capt Percival on 14 September 1937. During the initial flights with the undercarriage locked in the down position, some buffeting was experienced but overcome by the fitting of trouser-type

46

fairings. It was also found that the fully-glazed cockpit canopy caused glare and discomfort so the roof panel was replaced by ply with small transparent lights at the sides to give some vision upwards.

During the certification trials at the Aeroplane and Armament Establishment, Martlesham Heath, it was found that during the landing approach the flaps gradually closed. When the fault was investigated it was found that the brackets securing the flaps to the torque-tube were reliant upon friction only – the taper-pins which provided a positive lock had not been fitted! These were quickly inserted and the Certificate of Airworthiness was issued on 1 February 1938.

Initially five aircraft were built to the prototype standard and could be readily identified by the uniform spacing of the cabin windows. The prototype, K20, sporting the company's livery of torquoise-blue and silver was used as a demonstration aircraft and became a 'star' in a number of films. It remained with the company until 6 March 1940 when it left Luton to 'join up' as X9328. It survived the rigours of service use and was restored to the Civil Register in May 1945, first with Southern Aircraft (Gatwick) Ltd and then, two years later, with C. G. M. Alington. It returned to Luton in April 1951 in the ownership of W. J. Twitchell with whom it remained for a further six years before being sold to J. B. Peak and based at Cambridge. It was withdrawn from use in May 1959 and was last seen (by myself) standing forlornly, minus the tailplane, elevator and escape hatch, by the side of a hangar at Cranfield in Bedfordshire.

The second aircraft (Q21) was purchased by Sir Philip Sassoon and it

Built for the Australian Air Board, VH-ABY (Q35) was the third aircraft to be fitted with a retractable undercarriage (Flight).

was registered to him as G-AFFD on 6 April 1938 although records show that he took delivery of the aeroplane on 2 March 1938 at Lympne, remaining in his service until impressed in April 1940 as X9407. This also survived the war and was restored to the register when it was operated by the Yorkshire Aeroplane Club at Sherburn-in-Elmet until being sold in April 1952 to Walter Instruments Ltd of Redhill. In August 1956 it was serving as an instructional airframe at the Redhill College of Aeronautical Engineering. It was found again at Duxford lying in the open and acquired by the Midland Aircraft Museum and stored under cover at a Warwickshire farm. It was in an appalling condition but, by May 1983, much restoration had been undertaken and a new wing constructed by Speedwell Sailplanes of Marple in Cheshire.

The third machine, Q22, was purchased by King Ghazi of Iraq with the registration YI-ROH and Q23 as G-AFFE by H. B. Legge and Sons of Warlingham and based at Hansey Green. During the war it served with the Royal Navy being impressed in September 1939 as W9374. It was destroyed on 16 July 1940 during an air raid at Lee-on-Solent.

The fifth aeroplane built to the prototype standard was F-AQOK (Q24) which was sold to Leon Sternberg de Armella. It returned to Great Britain on 15 June 1938 flying in the overall yellow livery with black markings of Western Airways Ltd of Western-super-Mare until May 1940 when it joined the Royal Navy as AX860 and was based at Lee-on-Solent.

When delivered, 'factory fresh' to their first owners, the livery of each aircraft varied to the customer's choice. G-AFFD supplied to Sir Philip Sassoon was painted grey and silver with a gold-plated model of a cobra mounted just in front of the windscreen, F-AQOK chocolate-brown and cream but the most flamboyant was YI-ROH of King Ghazi. This was finished in a startling red and yellow. The fuselage, fin and rudder were in red and the rest of the aircraft yellow. A yellow flash ran from nose to tail through the registration letters with the name 'Bird of Eden' inscribed in copper-plate lettering just above the flash and beneath the cockpit windows. On the yellow cowlings red crowns were painted.

With the exception of 'EYE, all of these aircraft carried radio equipment, the mast being mounted on the top of the fuselage just aft of the cockpit with the aerial stretching from it to a bracket on the fin. A trailing aerial was located between the spars and protruded through the bottom of the fuselage.

From Q25 onwards the spar centres were increased and, as the position of the fuselage frames and, therefore, the windows was determined by this, the cabin windows varied in size and spacing. The nose was changed to a

The pleasing lines of the Q6 are well displayed in this photograph of the aircraft supplied to King Ghazi of Iraq (Flight).

49

P5636 makes a low pass. For some reason most of the RAF aircraft suffered from cooling problems and additional cooling louvres were inserted in the top cowlings at the leading edge of the wing to overcome this (Flight).

monocoque structure, the frames being overlaid with strips of thin plywood, about 4 inches wide, glued into position at 45° to each other. The first machine built to this standard, Q25, was initially registered as VH-ABL, built to the order of Capt P. G. Taylor who was a famous Australian pilot and navigator. It was the first of the type to be fitted with a retractable undercarriage and during the flight trials it was found necessary to increase the area of the elevator.

During a subsequent test flight to assess the improvement, gentle dives and climbs were being performed when the tail-plane fittings failed leaving that unit virtually fully floating! In other circumstances the aircraft may have been lost but, being in the capable hands of Capt Percival, a safe landing was made at base by using the trim-tabs. After rectification VH-ABL was sent to the Aeroplane and Armament Establishment for trials on the undercarriage. On its return it was not delivered to Australia but went instead to Vickers-Armstrong carrying the registration G-AFMT. In April 1940 it was impressed as X9454 but did not survive the war as on 10 September 1941, seventeen months after being drafted, it was damaged beyond repair in a crash at Castletown.

Lord Londonderry of Newtownards, a Director of Percival Aircraft Ltd, purchased Q26 and it was registered to him as G-AFGH on 26 June 1938 and Intava Ltd took possession of Q27 on 13 July of the same year the aircraft being registered G-AFGX. Eighteen months later both were impressed, G-AFGH as X9329 in February 1940 and G-AFGX a month later and given the serial X9336. It is believed that four months after being impressed G-AFGH was abandoned in France.

The next two aircraft (Q28 & Q29) were ordered by the Lithuanian airline 'Lietuvos Linijos' and given the registrations LY-SOA and LY-SOB. Two pilots of the airline were sent to collect them and after a period of instruction with the 'old man', both made solo flights on their respective aeroplanes. Unfortunately one of them had difficulty in adjusting to the lighter configurations of the machine and for almost an hour proceeded to demonstrate the robustness of his aircraft by executing a series of landings which would have been perfect had the ground been several feet higher! Jack Lavender, the Service Manager, uttering unprintable expletives and consuming quantities of whisky obtained from the bar of the Luton Flying Club, watched the proceedings with anguish as the pilot had yet to sign the papers of acceptance and the aircraft was still technically the responsibility of the company!

Vickers Aviation Ltd of Brooklands purchased Q30 and on 16 September 1938 it was registered to them as G-AFIW and used as a company 'hack' by them throughout the war still carrying its civil registration. After the war it was sold to J. Brochhouse & Co Ltd of Bromwich but later based at Minworth. In April 1947 it was acquired by Lt Cdr R. E. Bibby until September 1949 when it was returned to Luton where it was scrapped.

A retractable undercarriage was fitted to Q31 which, as G-AFIX, was delivered to Western Airways Ltd in a livery of red and blue on 12 December 1938. During the summer of 1939 it was used on the Castle Bromwich to Cardiff route over which the company operated. In April the ownership was changed to A. H. White of Luton although the aircraft continued to fly with Western Airways Ltd until it was impressed as X9406 in April 1940. During its service life the retractable undercarriage was removed and replaced by a fixed one. It was in this form that G-AFIX returned to civil life in May 1946

The prototype Q6 G-AEYE seen here in its post-war blue and white livery. The first five aircraft had equally spaced cabin windows.

when, for six months, it was used by the London & Oxford Steel Co Ltd. It was purchased by Freemantle Overseas Radio Ltd and served with them until it passed to Starways Ltd of Speke in May 1949 being used as a joyriding and taxi aircraft until written-off in a crash at Broomhall on 6 May 1949.

Q32, first registered as G-AFKG to L. A. Horden and Q33 registered to Lt Col E. T. Peel as G-AFKC and based at Almaza, Cairo, were both impressed; the former as X9363 and the latter as W6085. This was scrapped at Heliopolis in September 1941 nineteen months after it had been requisitioned. Q34 was already in the Royal Air Force having gone into service straight from the production line with the serial number P5638.

The third aircraft to be fitted with the retractable undercarriage was VH-ABY (Q35) for the Australian Air Board and Q36 went to India as VT-AKU being fitted with a conventional fixed undercarriage. After being registered to Viscount Forbes on 5 April 1939 and based at Croydon Q37 was impressed in December 1941 at Heliopolis. It was known to be flying in North Africa in September 1943 but further history has not come to hand.

The last civil aircraft to be built was Q38 which went to India as VT-AKR; the remaining six machines all entering military service straight from the production line. The Royal Air Force took delivery of Q39 to Q42, Q45 and Q46 (the last of the type to be constructed) where they served as P5634 to P5637, P5639 and P5640 respectively while the Royal Egyptian Air Force received Q43 and Q44 which served as Q601 and Q602.

After the war, P5637 that had entered the Royal Air Force on 18 August 1940 and used by the Woodley Communications Flight, was refurbished by Whitney Straight Ltd of Weston-super-Mare and given the registration G-AHOM and delivered to Denham in Buckinghamshire where it was flown by A. R. Lewis of Airway's Individual Reservations Ltd on a number of long-distance charter flights to Italy and North Africa. On the Christmas Eve of 1946 while flying from Le Bourget to Lympne in poor visibility 'HOM had to make an emergency landing at Jury's Gap near Dungeness and was severely damaged.

The remains were transported to Weston-super-Mare where the aeroplane was reconstructed to fly once again, this time with the Yellow Air Taxi Co (Midlands) Ltd with whom it served for a year. In June 1948 it left Elmdon, where it was based, and flown to Wolverhampton where it was operated by Ductile Steels Ltd until August 1953. It then returned to its designer, Capt E. W. Percival, who had returned to the aircraft construction business and was engaged in the development of his agricultural and general purpose aeroplane, the EP4. He retained 'HOM until the January of '58 when it was sold to Central Newbury Motors Ltd of Thruxton but it was withdrawn from use in the following July and finally dismantled in 1961.

P5634 and P5640 were also refurbished by Whitney Straight Ltd and both were sold to the London and Oxford Steel Co Ltd; P5640 as G-AHTA being registered on 27 July 1946 and P5634 as G-AHTB on 25 April of the following year. 'HTA remained with the London and Oxford Steel Co Ltd

for a short time only, as in the November of the same year (1946) it was delivered to COGEA, Brussels, carrying the registration OO-PQA. Five months after it had been acquired, G-AHTB was sold to S. E. Norman of Southend (in September) but two months later, on 2 November 1947 it was damaged beyond repair when landing at Almaza, Cairo.

For reason of economy, the works would incorporate the modifications required by the customer under verbal instructions from the design office. When these had been incorporated, we junior draughtsmen had to prepare the record drawings. As the aeroplane could not be released to the customer until these had been completed and approved, it was necessary to work fast and accurately. I had just completed one such set when, on the final check, I found to my horror that I had made a major error! Having made good progress on the job I had sufficient time to re-draw the offending detail but before submitting the work to my section leader it was necessary to answer an urgent call of nature. On returning to my drawing board I casually picked up one of the duplicated drawings and destroyed it – unfortunately it was the wrong one! For what seemed hours I chased my heart from mouth to boots and back again before restoring it to its rightful place! I have never worked so hard before or since to complete a job on time – even then I was reprimanded for being careless!

During the summer of 1938, Arthur Tyte, the foreman of the workshops reported that, due to a design fault, the structure supporting the fabric fairing the centre section spars into the fuselage did not fit. This puzzled me somewhat as, having done the drawings, the fault had not been reported on previous builds. When I inspected the offending machine the answer was obvious! The light ¼ inch × ½ inch stringers which were originally specified had grown to massive ½ inch × 1 inch timbers! I quizzed the 'chippie' who was doing the work and he admitted that he had lost or mislaid his copy of the drawing so, to be on the safe side, had progressively 'added a bit' to each dimension on subsequent builds!

Three of a kind, LY-SOB the second Lietuvos Oro Linijos aircraft, VH-ABL of the Australian Air Board and G-AFGX of Intava which was impressed as X9336 in March 1940 (Harold Cox).

Although fitted with a fixed undercarriage, this head-on view of LY-SOA shows the clean lines of the aeroplane (Harold Cox).

The skill of Capt Percival when confronted with an emergency was demonstrated to Harold Curtis, my section leader during a flight in G-AEYE. Due to incorrect wire locking, a fuel filter loosened causing an air-lock in the fuel system. This resulted in a total loss of power during take-off. In this incident it was not possible to return to base as had been earlier in VH-ABL so an emergency landing was made in a field on the side of a hill near the, now non-existent, Chiltern Green Railway Station not far from Luton. The descent of the stricken machine was observed by Jack Lavender who gathered a couple of his engineers and followed at high speed in his car. At the scene of the landing he was confronted by an irate Percival who needed a considerable amount of cooling down! After rectification the machine was flown out, which, in itself was no mean feat of flying. When recounting the episode back in the office, Curtis maintained that his only concern was where to hang on. At the time only the pilot's seat had been fitted so he had to sit on the spar!

This incident and that with 'ABL were the only incidents – apart from a scare when, in 1938, Percival used 'EYE for a weekend visit to the Continent. He changed his destination without informing anyone. For 24 hours he was reported missing and the newspapers made hay with such headlines as . . . 'FAMOUS AVIATOR MISSING' and 'PERCIVAL MISSING ON FLIGHT TO CONTINENT'. Percival, as Queen Victoria, was not amused!

While I was gathering information from G-AEYE on another occasion, Capt Percival entered the cabin and it was quite obvious that he was about to fly so I began to collect my equipment together prior to vacating the machine. This was noted by Percival who then instructed me to continue with my work. Needless to say, this was not possible so I made myself comfortable and enjoyed the flight!

One further anecdote before closing this narrative on the 'Q' machines. One of them had radio direction finding equipment fitted and it was necessary for this to be 'set-up' so an engineer was sent from the manufacturing company. He arranged that Percival should fly the aircraft around the Brookmans Park transmitter and as communication between the two while in flight was not practical, requested that the transmitter should be circled for about twenty minutes, this being considered sufficient time for the engineer to complete his task. Upon reaching the masts, Percival proceeded to circle as agreed – but in a square configuration with vertical banks producing high 'G' forces at each change of direction. After the prescribed time, Percival headed for home where, after landing, he enquired if the engineer had completed his task satisfactorily. 'No,' came the reply . . . 'I was too busy trying not to be sick!'

In the late summer of 1937 a further two bays were added to those existing which made it possible for both works and offices to be under the same roof. Prior to this visits to the workshops from our haven in the farmhouse entailed ploughing through a sea of mud ankle-deep.

The Drawing Office was housed in one corner and separated from the workshops by a partition and offices of wood and hardboard. Aeroplane hangars are inhabited by birds and the partition was not bird-proof so henceforth, until we took up residence in the office block in 1939, all our drawings were soiled by bird droppings.

During the following years the workshops expanded to treble their original size. This was later to cause problems for the Works Engineer. No increase had been made to the original rain-water drains which, although more than adequate for their original purpose, were quite unable to cope with the water being channelled into them from the increased roof area. Furthermore, the manhole covers giving access to the drains were now in the middle of the new bays. During heavy rain a back-pressure was formed in the inadequate pipes which forced off the covers and flooded the shops to a depth of several inches. When this happened the Works Engineer simply shook his head, looked wise and muttered 'freak conditions . . . that's what it is . . . freak conditions!'

Mew Gull G-AEKL which was to have been flown by Campbell-Black in the Schlesinger race. Shortly after this photograph was taken the cockpit area was destroyed when a Hawker Hart taxied into it killing Campbell-Black (Flight).

The prototype Mew Gull, G-ACND, after being fitted with a modified undercarriage. Compare this with the photograph on page 58 (via Hugh Scanlan).

CHAPTER 4

THE MEW GULL

In the corner of the workshops and covered by a tarpaulin were the remains of a Mew Gull bearing the registration G-AEKL. Tom Campbell-Black had intended to fly the machine in the Schlesinger Air Race to Johannesburg to be flown in the late September and early October of 1936. On 19 September he had flown the aircraft to Speke for a ceremony during which the machine was named 'Miss Liverpool', but while waiting to take-off a Hawker Hart, the pilot not having seen the diminutive Mew Gull, taxied into it and the airscrew reduced the cockpit to matchwood killing the unfortunate Campbell-Black. The remains had been acquired by Charles Gardner who had it rebuilt for the 1937 Kings Cup Air Race. When it emerged from the workshops the original livery of white overall with a black top to the fuselage and black lettering had been replaced by a resplendent maroon finish with gold lettering, wing tips and flashes along the fuselage and undercarriage fairings. At the same time a new version was being built.

Allocated the design letter 'E', the Mew Gull first flew in March 1934. It was a small racing monoplane with a wing span of only 24 ft and a length of 18 ft 3 in. At that time it was extremely fast – faster in fact than the contemporary fighter aircraft – and was the first civil aeroplane to exceed 200 miles an hour!

The wooden structure followed the pattern established in the Gull, the fuselage being a plywood box stiffened by spruce longerons and frames enclosed at the top and bottom by curved plywood deckings supported on laminated spruce frames. The top decking merged into the fin and the enclosed cockpit, fitted with a windscreen of flat panels, was accessible through hinged side and roof panels and situated aft of the wing.

The power unit, originally a Napier Javelin of 165 hp (later changed for a de Havilland Gipsy Six of 200 hp) driving a Fairey metal airscrew was mounted on tubular steel bearers bolted to the front of the fuselage and isolated by a bulkhead of aluminium/asbestos sandwich. Thirty gallons of fuel were carried in two tanks mounted between the two close-set spars of the ply-covered wing which was built as a single unit.

As on the Gull, the two-spar tailplane could be adjusted in flight by a cable operated screw-jack. All the control surfaces were fabric covered and all flying controls were enclosed within the structure.

The undercarriage units were identical to those fitted to the Gull Series 1 & 2 and due to the comparatively large fairings needed to enclose them, the aircraft gained the nickname of the 'Beetle in Boots'. In this form the machine was first flown in March 1934 by Capt Percival and found to be

The compact lines of G-ACND in its original form powered by a Napier Javelin engine driving a Fairey metal airscrew are well depicted in this photograph (Percival Aircraft Ltd).

rather sensitive in the longitudinal plane. Shortly afterwards the undercarriage was changed to the smaller semi-cantilever type with neat wheel spats which made the aircraft look rather like a well-bosomed dowager marchioness tottering about on spindly legs!

It was entered in the 1935 King's Cup flown from Hatfield on 13 July during which it lapped the course at a remarkable average speed of 191 mph. While competing in the Coupe Michelin Event toward the end of October of the same year, fog was encountered while flying between Bordeaux and Orly forcing the pilot, Comte Guy de Chateubrun who was Percival's agent in France, to abandon the aircraft. It was totally destroyed in the ensuing crash near Angouleme.

During its rebuild for which it was allocated the construction number E20A (the original aircraft had been allocated the construction number E20), the opportunity was taken to incorporate a vast number of design changes suggested by Arthur Bage and although the original registration number was retained it was an entirely new aeroplane.

Designated the E2H, the fuselage was increased by two feet which gave an overall length of 20 ft 3 in, and the flat panels of the windscreen were replaced by a moulded unit with flutes on either side of the instrument panel to improve the pilot's somewhat restricted forward view.

At the front end a de Havilland Gipsy Six engine of 200 hp driving a Fairey-Reed fixed-pitch airscrew provided the motive power. As an alternative a de Havilland Gipsy Six Series II was offered and, indeed, fitted to all subsequent Mew Gulls. To aid cooling eighteen louvres were inserted in the starboard side-panel of the engine cowling.

The tailplane became a fixed ply-covered unit rigidly mounted on brackets bolted to the top longerons; trimming being by an in-flight adjustable tab in the port elevator. All control surfaces had single spars of spruce and ply, spruce ribs, aluminium tube trailing edges and were fabric-covered. With the exception of the elevator, all were mass-balanced by external weights.

The re-stressed wing carried an increased fuel capacity of 48½ gallons in two tanks mounted between the wing spars and inboard of the under-carriage units which were neatly faired cantilever components with hydraulic damping and were mounted in prefabricated steel brackets bolted to the front spar. The span of the wing had increased by a nominal 9 inches giving a new span of 24 ft 9 in and the wing area had been enlarged from 78 sq ft to 88.5 sq ft. The all-up weight had also increased by 255 lb (from 1,545 lb to 1,800 lb) with a resultant increase in the wing loading of 3.2 lb/sq ft (from 19.8 to 23 lb/sq ft). The power loading increased by 1.08 lb/hp, giving a total loading of 8.8 lb/hp. In later versions of the E2H there was a further increase in the all-up weight mainly due to the installation of the Gipsy Six Series II engine equipped with the variable-pitch airscrew. This increase to 2,125 lb gave a power loading of 10.35 lb/hp and a wing loading of 25.6 lb/sq ft.

Although a heavier aircraft, the performance had improved remarkably. The maximum speed had been raised to 225 mph, an improvement of some 21 mph, and the cruising speed had gone up from 180 to 190 mph. In its original form the Mew Gull had landed at 65 mph but by fitting split trailing-edge flaps this had been reduced to 58 mph. With the Series II engine

After the E2H Mew Gull G-AEKL had been rebuilt following the tragic accident at Speke, it was flown by Charles Gardner into first place in the King's Cup Air Race of 1937 (C. W. Rogers).

The Mew Gull flown by
Major A. M. Miller in the
Schlesinger Race cavorts
among the clouds. It was
sold to Alex Henshaw and
extensively modified by John
Cross (Percival Aircraft
Ltd).

driving a variable pitch airscrew a further increase in the maximum speed
was achieved, it increased to 235 mph, as was the cruising speed which was
raised to 220 mph. The landing speed, however, increased slightly to
60 mph.

On 1 July 1935 the redesigned Mew Gull made its debut at the SBAC
show held at Hendon. After the show it was quickly fitted with a Regnier
engine of 180 hp as a temporary measure to qualify for entry into the Coup
Armand Esders flown over a course from Deauville to Cannes and back, a
total distance of 1,046 miles. Flown by Comte Guy de Chateaubrun who had
had such a traumatic experience in the previous aeroplane, the Mew Gull
averaged 188 mph over the complete course to win this premier award.

On its return to England the Mew Gull was returned to its original form
with the Gipsy Six engine and entered in the King's Cup with Percival as the
pilot. It was unfortunate that Percival always seemed to attract the
unwanted attentions of the handicappers who invariably thought that he
had 'something up his sleeve'. Although in the 1935 race Percival lapped at
an average speed of 208.9 mph and in doing so established the record of
being the first ever to exceed 200 mph in that annual event, he could not
overcome the penalty imposed by the handicappers and could only gain
sixth place. Percival fared better in the Folkstone Trophy race later in the
year when, at an average speed of 198.5 mph, he gained third place. Success
came in the Heston to Cardiff Race which was won at a creditable average
speed of 218 mph.

In 1936 three further Mew Gulls were built, the first, E21, being
registered to Percival Aircraft on 30 June with the registration G-AEKL and

flown by Capt Percival in the King's Cup and Folkestone Trophy Air Races. In the King's Cup Percival achieved the fastest time of the day but needless to say, the handicappers made sure that he could not win! After these races the machine was purchased by Air Publicity Ltd of Heston who had it fitted with additional fuel tanks in preparation for the forthcoming Schlesinger Race during which it was to have been flown by Campbell-Black, the tragic story of whom has been told at the beginning of this chapter.

After being owned and flown by Charles Gardner in a number of races, 'ELK passed to Giles Guthrie who also flew it with some success in many competitions. It was then sold to Jimmy Mollison who had the aircraft resprayed in a livery of overall black (Mollison's favourite colour) with red lettering outlined in gold. The name 'Southern Cloud' was inscribed in copperplate lettering on the engine cowlings. Mollison did not have the chance to exploit his latest acquisition as, soon after, war was declared and all civil flying was banned. The Mew Gull was put into storage for the duration of hostilities at Lympne but during an air raid in 1940 the aeroplane was destroyed.

The two other Mew Gulls were both ordered by veteran South African pilots and entered in the Schlesinger Race, E22 being registered to Major A. M. Miller as ZS-AHM on 11 September and E23 to Capt S. S. Halse as ZS-AHO two days later. Prior to the race ZS-AHO was temporarily re-registered as G-AEMO. Both machines sported the standard company livery of off-white with dark blue lettering and both were named, ZS-AMH as the 'Golden City' and ZS-AHO 'Baragwanath'; the names being inscribed in copperplate lettering on the engine cowlings.

During the race Capt Halse made a meteoric dash southwards but on 31 September was forced to land the aircraft near Bomobohawa in Southern Rhodesia. In doing so the machine ran into a large ant-hill, turned over on

Following its destruction, 'CND was redesigned and re-built to become the fore runner of an outstanding line of racing monoplanes (Flight).

The last Mew Gull to be built was G-AFAA seen here at Hatfield when participating in the 1937 King's Cup (C. W. Rogers).

its back and was extensively damaged. Attention from the ants did not improve matters! Major Miller was also unlucky. He ran out of fuel and was forced to make a dead-stick landing when within sight of the first control at Belgrade. After replenishing his tanks with low-grade spirit he managed to reach Belgrade but retired and returned to England where, on 11 September the aircraft was re-registered as G-AEXF and sold to Alex Henshaw of which more will be told later.

At the same time as G-AEKL was being rebuilt, a new aircraft was being constructed. Although Percival had always achieved the fastest time when flying a Mew Gull in the King's Cup he had yet to win that coveted trophy and it was for that reason a new version, the E3H model, was designed and built. It bore a strong resemblance to the previous models but was stressed for a much higher level of performance.

The taper of the wing was reduced from the former ratio of 1.8 to 2.1 and the area was decreased from 88.5 sq ft to 75 sq ft, achieved by reducing the wing span to 22 ft 9 in. The aerofoil section was also modified with a reduced camber further aft and a sharper leading edge.

The frontal area was also reduced, the width of the fuselage being determined by the dimensions of Percival's frame. As on previous models, the ubiquitous de Havilland Series II engine provided the motive power through a de Havilland constant-speed airscrew with limited pitch variation of 9° but, to accommodate the exceptionally wide speed range, this was later increased to 12°. To reduce the frontal area to a minimum, the air-intake was positioned in the nose cowling with a duct to transport the air to the carburettor and the undercarriage fairings were made to fit more closely.

A fuel tank of 16 gallons capacity was fitted in the fuselage between the cockpit and firewall while the wing tanks, still mounted between the spars, were reduced to 11 gallons each.

Prior to receiving its full certificate of airworthiness, the E3H was flown in red mainoxide and bore the class B registration X2, the classification X1 being used at that time by the Q6. During the flight it was established that the maximum speed had increased to 245 mph and the cruising speed pushed up to 230 mph. The all-up weight had increased to 1,850 lb which gave a wing loading of 24.5 lb/sq ft but the landing speed still remained at 60 mph.

A single louvre had been fitted at the rear of the starboard side panel of the engine cowling but this was found to be unnecessary and removed. The aeroplane was given the standard Mew Gull livery of off-white but the blue lettering was outlined in gold as were flash-lines on the fuselage and undercarriage fairings.

It was registered on 6 September 1937, as G-AFAA and entered by Lady Wakefield for the King's Cup Air Race of that year. In the eliminating stages of the contest flown over a course from Hatfield to Dublin via Aberdeen, Percival averaged 225.5 mph in appalling weather conditions to gain the Wakefield prize of £200 for the fastest time by an aeroplane powered by an engine exceeding 150 hp.

On the following day the final course from Dublin to Hatfield via Carlisle, Leicester and Cardiff was completed by Percival at an average speed of 238.7 mph which, although the fastest time failed to overcome the handicap, placed Percival in second place, the coveted first place being awarded to Charles Gardner who had completed the course in his rebuilt E2H Mew Gull at an average speed of 233.7 mph. Earlier in the year the Newcastle Air Race had been won by Gardner at an average speed of 221 mph and the Folkestone Trophy by Henshaw who lapped the course at an average speed of 210 mph both, of course, were flying their Mew Gulls.

Further modifications were made to 'FAA for the 1938 competitions. The cross-section of the engine cowling was reduced still further and the carburettor air-intake pipe, still in the nose cowling, was placed closer to the airscrew to give a form of supercharging. The overall frontal area was also reduced by lowering the height of the rear coaming and canopy. The height of the canopy was determined, after the existing structure had been removed, by sitting Percival in the cockpit with a lath, supported on a post, passing over his head to the forward decking.

The post was progressively reduced in height until the minimum clearance had been achieved. After several inches had been removed from the post, the lath then being quite close to Percival's head, one of the workmen leaned forward and suggested that . . . 'if the Captain would care to remove his hat we could gain several more inches'. No man could have made a more rash request! Captain Percival never flew without his famous brown trilby, in fact the press would report that 'the HAT attended such-and-such meeting accompanied by that well known aviator Captain Percival'.

The effect of that request was electrifying . . . there was a brief silence before Percival exploded. 'You can have the bloody cushion', he roared, lifting himself up and throwing out that item . . . 'you can have the bloody parachute', that followed the cushion . . . 'but you're not having my bloody hat!' The Hat stayed!

As the constant-speed airscrew then fitted had a pitch variation of 12° whereas a variation of 14° was now necessary to accommodate the full speed range of the revised Mew Gull, for the King's Cup Race of 1938 the propeller was adjusted to give maximum take-off performance. This had an adverse effect on the acceleration and maximum speed.

The course for that year was from Hatfield via Buntingford to Barton-le-Clay and back to Hatfield, a distance of 50.607 miles which had to be flown twenty times in four stages of five laps each. In all some sixty turns had to be made and between each stage there was a compulsory refuelling period.

With no eliminating race the handicap times were based on estimated performance figures which, from previous experience, did not bode well for Percival; he became scratch man and it was not until the first aircraft to take off had been airborne for 2¾ hours did he enter the race. Although almost two minutes were gained on the handicap at each stage, E. W. P. could only achieve sixth place at an average speed fo 234 mph, some 2 mph slower than the winner, Alex Henshaw in his much modified E2H Mew Gull. This broke Percival's run of establishing the fastest time of the day.

At that time we were required to work on Saturday mornings and that Saturday in 1938 – King's Cup or not – was to be the same as any other Saturday in spite of requesting time off. The Captain would have none of it! As the course from Barton-le-Clay to Hatfield passed close to Luton Airport we were able to observe the competitors from the office windows therefore little useful work was done during that morning!

When it was seen that E. W. P. had joined the race and could no longer interfere, Arthur Bage – who was equally as keen to get away to Hatfield – dismissed us. Having no means of transport, a number of us walked a short distance to a better vantage point. When 'FAA next passed overhead we noted a slight deviation in the flight path and a lowering of the wing. We understood the significance of this on the following Monday when a number of us were summoned to the office of an irate Percival and

reprimanded for disobeying his instructions!

Further minor modifications were incorporated in 1939, the nose cowling was increased in slope in the side elevation and an airscrew was supplied by de Havillands which had sufficient pitch variation to enable the E3H to achieve its full potential of 264 mph. In the London to the Isle of Man race of 1939 Percival, once again, established the fastest time at an average speed of 220 mph but could only achieve third place as oil leaking from the crank-case had obscured his vision and had caused him to fly wide at the finishing post.

In the Manx Derby flown on the following day Percival once again returned the fastest time at an average speed of 237 mph but was beaten into second place by Albert 'Pop' Henshaw, Alex's father, who was flying a Vega Gull, the time between the two aeroplanes at the finishing line being 44 seconds.

During the war G-AFAA was loaned to de Havillands and while being flown by one of their test pilots it stalled on landing and dropped from a considerable height. The impact with the ground drove the undercarriage legs through the wings and did other major damage. The remains were returned to Luton but, it is sad to relate, after the war this remarkable and attractive aircraft ended its career as the 'star' of a fire-fighting display together with the wing of G-ACND, the only remaining component of its illustrious predecessor.

To complete the story of the Mew Gull it is necessary to return to 1938. In that year Alex Henshaw's G-AEKL was fitted with a de Havilland Gipsy Six R engine (originally fitted to the de Havilland DH88 Comet, G-ACSS which had won the Australian Air Race) driving a Ratier variable-pitch airscrew of French design and manufacture; the work being done by Herts

Entered by Major Miller in the Schlesinger race, ZS-AHM was re-registered G-AEXF and sold to Alex Henshaw. It became the longest surviving Mew Gull (Flight).

and Essex Aero Ltd at Gravesend under the direction of John Cross. At the same time, much to the disgust of Capt Percival, the top decking, cockpit, engine cowlings and undercarriage fairings were drastically modified reducing a once elegant aeroplane into an ugly, but nevertheless, efficient flying machine.

To conform to the regulations governing entry for the King's Cup, the aircraft was fitted with a de Havilland constant-speed airscrew on a short extension shaft. Henshaw won the race at an average speed fo 236.25 mph, which was also the fastest time of the day, with Guthrie in second place, Percival gaining sixth place.

The machine was then returned to Gravesend for further grooming by John Cross who fitted it with a de Havilland Gipsy Six Series II engine, long-range tanks and a radio which increased the all-up weight to 2,350 lb. On 5 February 1939 Henshaw took-off from Gravesend on the historical flight to Capetown and back which was completed in the record time of 4 days 10 hr 16 min. Flying conditions were terrible and the aeroplane was subjected to violent buffeting which caused injury to Henshaw.

In the following June the Mew Gull was sold to a Frenchman who, during World War II, stored it in a shed north of Lyons where it remained undetected by occupying German forces until 1950, eleven years later, when it was rediscovered by H. E. Scrope. On 2 July, with no previous experience of flying a Mew Gull and with a sick engine, Scrope flew the machine non-stop from Bron to Blackbushe aerodrome.

In August of the following year, 'EXF was involved in a landing accident at Shoreham and during the subsequent rebuild by D. E. Bianci the canopy was enlarged. After the work had been completed in 1953, the aeroplane was entered by J. N. Somers in the race for the Kemsley Trophy which was flown from Southend in June. A year later the canopy was again modified, this time by Adie Aviation Ltd at Croydon, who raised it still further. It was then entered by its new owner, Fred Dunkerley, in the King's Cup which was flown on 20 August 1955. With Peter Clifford as the pilot, the course was covered at an average speed of 213.5 mph which gave victory to the nineteen year old veteran.

It was then placed in store until it was flown to Yeadon on 29 October 1962 where J. E. G. Appleyard fitted a Gipsy Queen II engine which was originally installed in a Proctor III, G-ALFX. At the same time another canopy was fitted. In May of the following year the Mew Gull was involved in yet another taxying accident which damaged the undercarriage and this was replaced by units from a Proctor.

While being flown by E. Crabtree on 6 August 1965 during a practice session for the National Air Races, 'EXF made a forced landing at Catterick, Yorkshire, and was severely damaged, however, the wreckage was purchased by Martin Barraclough and Tom Storey in 1972 who, after many years of painstaking work, restored the venerable monoplane into a form closely resembling its original configuration. In late 1983 their pride and joy was again severely damaged by the propeller of a run-away Auster.

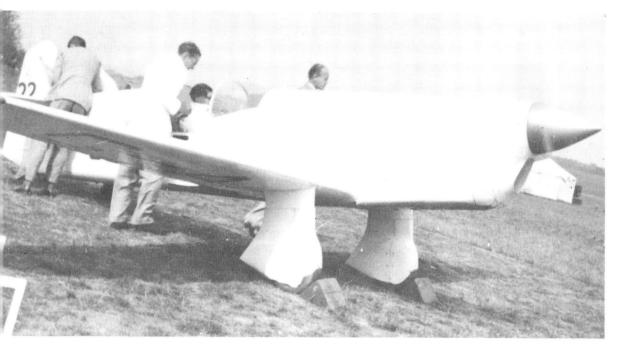

To his employees, Percival always tended to be irascible, particularly so when work was in progress on his beloved Mew Gull. At the drop of a hat he would fire the entire drawing office – or indeed anyone else causing him displeasure, real or imaginary! Usually this was ignored but on one occasion this instruction was complied with and the entire drawing office staff (at the instigation of the Senior Section Leaders) walked out making a lot of noise in the process, particularly when passing the door of the 'old mans' office.

Suddenly this was thrown open and we were confronted by the scowling figure of Percival. His rage errupted once again. 'What the bloody hell do you think you are doing?' he demanded, 'Get back to your drawing boards or it will be the worse for you!' Such was the effect that we all momentarily stopped in our tracks. 'Aw! Get lost' replied one of the ring leaders, 'we no longer work for you, you fired us. Remember?'

This rebuff completely put Percival off stride. His mouth opened and closed but no sound was forthcoming. By this time Arthur Bage had arrived on the scene and managed to persuade us to do as we had been bidden, an easy task as at that time jobs were hard to come by. Nevertheless, we had made our point and thereafter Percival tended to treat us with greater respect.

This respect, however, did not extend to matters of design. When assisting Harold Curtis in plotting the revised lines for the fuselage of the E3H Mew Gull, Percival was called in (as was usual) to approve the result. He took one look and rounded on Harold. 'You haven't an idea when it comes to lines Curtis,' he commented extracting a thick-leaded pencil from his pocket, 'you've got a lump here, that needs fairing off,' the pencil

The much-modified E2H Mew Gull G-AEXF. Although the pleasing lines were destroyed by the attentions of John Cross it was, never-the-less, a very potent aeroplane (C. W. Rogers).

moved back and forth over the offending area producing a line at least ⅛ inch thick, 'you've got a hollow here,' more action from the pencil, 'and it's too bloody sharp here!' In the end our beautiful drawing was reduced to a shambles; covered by thick black scribbles. 'Put those right and I'll have another look in the morning.' With that Percival turned on his heels and swept out of the office.

'Blimme! That's a turn-up for the books!' I remarked, 'What's to be done now?' Harold gave me a knowing wink and waved his hand over the drawing. 'First we'll remove this rubbish,' he said pointing to the scribbles,' and then we will pick up the original lines again. I pricked the points so it should be an easy matter . . . after that I'm going to take the afternoon off. You can do the same if you wish.' I was rather taken aback at this. 'Won't the Captain be annoyed if we don't change the lines?' I queried. 'No,' came the reply, 'the old bugger won't known the difference!'

The following morning when Percival came to inspect our efforts his face was wreathed in smiles. 'There you are Curtis, I told you you knew sweet f . . . a . . about lines!' Harold merely looked at me and slowly lowered an eye-lid!

As a postscript, when we first started working on the E3H programme it had been intended that much of the construction would be completed using many of the E2H drawings but when these were withdrawn from the files it was discovered that mice – probably fugitives from the many demolished farm buildings – had taken residence in the drawers and, to make themselves comfortable quarters, had chewed the middle out of the drawings leaving, in most cases, only protective tape edge-bindings!

It is an interesting speculation that, had it not been for the activities of these small rodents the E3H may not have existed. I doubt that such a theory would receive official backing!

CHAPTER 5

THE PROCTORS

In 1938 things were well underway. The sales of the 'Q6' were healthy and the factory was engaged in meeting these orders and those for the Vega Gull. The production line included several of the latter which had been ordered by the Air Ministry. The clouds of war were gathering on the horizon and Capt Percival was negotiating with the Air Ministry to supply further Vega Gulls as communication aircraft. As the negotiations were progressing reasonably favourably, to meet the anticipated specification which was always issued when an aircraft was required for the services, a tentative redesign was undertaken under the design letter 'W'. A wind-tunnel model of the proposed design was made, but as the Vega Gull was eventually accepted with some modification to adapt it for military service, the project was shelved.

Two other interesting projects were undertaken during this period. One of them, a tandem two-seat trainer of which a mock-up was built, was designed under the design letter 'S' to meet the Air Ministry specification T1/37. It bore a strong resemblance to the Open gull but the project failed to attract support and was dropped. The other, allocated the design letter 'U', was an amphibian based on a Saro Cloud hull fitted with 'Q6' wings. The motive power was to have been supplied by two de Havilland Gipsy Six engines. A hull was delivered to Luton but no further work was undertaken.

The anticipated order and specification for the three seat radio trainer and communications aircraft based on the Vega Gull was received by the company during the late summer. The revised design, still retaining the

An early production model of the Proctor I. The engine cowlings are similar to those fitted to the civil Vega Gull and no oil cooler is fitted.

A three-quarter rear view of P6132 which was an early production aircraft. The square window at the rear of the cabin was hinged at the top and opened inwards allowing the radio operator (who was also required to navigate) to mount an external compass on the wedge plates at the top longerons.

design letter K, was to be known as the Proctor. The de Havilland Gipsy Queen engine of 205 hp was specified as the power unit and the airframe differed visually from its predecessor by having square windows at the rear of the cabin with a radio mast and DF loop mounted on the top decking above the doors, the latter being enclosed in a stream-lined clear plastic moulding.

Although fitted with navigation lamps those of the Vega Gull were of the sectored type mounted on the cabin roof and beneath the centre section. On the Proctor traditional lamps were fitted at the wing tips behind clear moulded fairings and on the rudder. Landing lamps were also fitted in the leading edges of both wings behind clear panels and three coloured identification lamps were installed in the bottom of the fuselage aft of the cabin.

Although structurally similar to the Vega Gull many detailed changes were necessary to convert the aircraft for military use. The rear floor of the cabin had to be strengthened to carry the loads imposed by the swivelling seat of the radio operator (on the Vega Gull the loads from the passenger's seat were transmitted to the fuselage walls) and sundry equipment disposed about the cabin floor. To provide the necessary rigidity, balsa wood was used as a filler between the structural members (and what a God-send were the off-cuts to the modelling fraternity!)

The locker at the rear of the cabin and its exterior door were increased in size to accommodate the T/R1082/83 radio installation with which the Proctor was initially equipped, the power to drive it being supplied by a large engine-driven generator mounted in brackets on the starboard frame of the engine bearers and covered by a large blister on the side cowling.

In the event of a ditching a three-man dinghy was fitted in the starboard side of the centre section aft of the rear spars within a, then novel, plastic container. The dinghy could be inflated automatically through an electrically-operated immersion switch or manually by a lever mounted between the seats on the centre section spar box. The cabin doors could also

be jettisoned in an emergency by withdrawing the hinge-pins by means of levers pivoted at the top of the laminated frame which supported the rear of the windscreen, the counter-balance cables and springs as fitted to the Vega Gull being removed.

It had been foreseen that, in the event of hostilities, it would be necessary to supplement the production capacity available at Luton by using sub-contractors. To meet this requirement it was necessary to revise the civilian method of working. Mass-production was envisaged whereby workers, either singly or in groups, would undertake one operation similar to the system operated in the motor industry. With this in mind the depleted staff, some sixteen in number (the rest being members of the RAFVR had been called to their squadrons) set to work to produce the necessary drawings.

To give some idea of the task, five drawings were required to manufacture a simple bracket compared with the one needed on the civilian counterpart. Each item or operation was detailed on separate drawings – flat plate development, gussets, reinforcing washers etc. while another gave the bending details and the final drawing the welding details. Where possible such items as ply gussets, clips, special bolts and washers were standardised. Even spruce members were scheduled in size, length and quantity for each machine.

This approach was totally alien to that used on civil aircraft where drawings were considered to be a necessary evil! This imposed quite a heavy load on the drawing office but spurred on by the promise of a bonus, and often working into the small hours, the task was completed in a little over six months and the first Proctor flew on 8 October 1939. When war did break out, components and even complete aircraft were made by sub-contractors, many being furniture manufacturers skilled in woodworking but with no

The centre section of the Proctor I. This particular centre section was for a Royal Air Force aeroplane as the container in the starboard side for stowing the dinghy is not fitted (Air Ministry).

experience of aircraft. They had little difficulty in the transition and eventually some 1,154 Proctors were produced.

Although the Gipsy Six Series II, the civil version of the Gipsy Queen, had behaved perfectly, running continuously for many hours during the long record making flights, high cylinder head and oil temperatures were experienced during the early flight trials of the Proctor. To rectify this the nose cowling was modified to improve the ram effect on the air passing over the cylinders and, to cope with the increased airflow, the rear of the bottom cowling panel was lowered. An oil cooler was also mounted in a tubular structure on the port undersurface of the centre section to supplement the surface cooling of the oil tank.

In service use it was found that, on prolonged flights, the nose would gradually rise although the aircraft had been correctly trimmed. A positive forward movement of the control column was required to correct the attitude. During the subsequent investigation it was found that the radio equipment tended to be a little over-weight and this, coupled with the long moment-arm, had caused the centre of gravity to move beyond its limits. The centre of gravity on Proctors tended to be rather critical and a warning notice was stencilled in large red letters on the inside of the doors to the cabin of all aircraft.

To restore the C of G to its correct position, the radio equipment was located in various positions and the crew was reduced to two. First, the equipment was mounted in a cradle in the rear of the cabin which was previously occupied by the radio operator who was relocated alongside the pilot in a rearward facing seat mounted on the spar box. In this form the aircraft was designated the Proctor I Series 1.

Next, the equipment was located alongside but forward of the pilot, the dual flying controls were removed and the centre section modified to provide a foot-well for the radio operator. His seat was mounted on bearers extending backwards from the rear spar. At the same time the signal pistol, which had been located beneath the coaming where it discharged forward and downward through a blast-tube, was moved to be more accessible from the new position of the radio operator and mounted in the floor of the foot-well. In this configuration the aircraft was designated the Proctor II.

A further version designated the Proctor III was produced in which the radio equipment was located alongside the pilot in a cradle; the radio operator being restored to his original position in the rear of the cabin. The designation of the various aircraft became a little confusing as, apart from the Proctor I which was fitted with dual controls, the only difference between the various marks was the disposition of the radio equipment – although there were some minor structural changes. It was therefore possible for one mark of aircraft to have its radio equipment located as in another with the exception of the Proctor I which, being fitted with dual controls, precluded the installation of the equipment as in the Proctor II. In these instances the mark number became a series number. For example, a Proctor II with the radio equipment disposed as in the Proctor III became a

Proctor II Series III etc.

After the fall of France when an invasion of the British Isles seemed imminent, an order was issued that all aircraft should be capable of operating in the offensive role. To comply, the Proctor was fitted with bomb racks under the centre section and fuselage to carry a load of sixteen 20 lb bombs, the entire programme from initial design to the final installation and flight trials being completed in less than three weeks. I was one of the draughtsmen engaged on this task and the drawing office had just moved into the recently completed administration block. As the building had yet to be 'blacked-out', a temporary inner office was quickly erected in which we worked during the hours of darkness. With little or no ventilation and all of us smoking heavily to sustain our powers of concentration, a first-class fug quickly developed! This entailed frequent excursions to the clear air outside to refresh ourselves!

Bill Shakespear, the dope-shop foreman and a former airship coxwain, tended to be rather irascible and was feared by the younger members of the

A post-war civil Proctor flying in the colours of the Vega Gulls supplied to the Air Ministry before the war. The modification to the air-intake in the nose cowling and the lowered bottom panel to improve cylinder cooling are clearly seen as is the oil cooler mounted under the centre section. A slinger-ring was also fitted around the nose cowling to prevent oil escaping from the airscrew fouling the windscreen (Air Portraits).

The leather upholstery on the walls and carpets on the floor identifies this shot of the Proctor Mk I cabin as a pre-war aeroplane. The switch at the bottom of the windscreen selected and operated the ident lamps mounted in the bottom of the fuselage.

The T/R 1154/55 radio installation in the rear locker of the Proctor Mk I. The 'Y' shaped tube stowed on the cabin wall above the fire extinguisher was the control locking device (Royal Aircraft Establishment).

company although I found him to be friendly and very interesting. I spent many lunch hours with him when he would tell me about his early experiences, particularly those on the ill fated R101, built by Short Bros Ltd at nearby Cardington. Because of his concern with the condition of the gas-bags he had refused to fly on what was to be its last tragic flight. For this he was placed on a court martial but the charge was dropped after the crash.

A little light relief from the interminable application of drab camouflage paint was given to Shakespear when, in 1941, a Proctor I was ordered to be finished in a pale metallic blue livery by an Air Commodore who wished to use the machine as his personal aircraft. Bill took a special interest in the job, undertaking much of the work himself and when the resplendent aeroplane was moved to the flight shed for its pre-delivery checks it went with the warning that, should any harm befall it, he, Bill Shakespear, would personally tear the culprit limb from limb . . . and as he operated on a very short fuse would be most likely to carry out such a threat!

An official photograph of the Proctor IV Fleet Air Arm version then known as the T9/41 (Air Ministry).

It so happened that, during the pre-flight checks, it was found necessary to change the battery. This was mounted on the cabin floor behind the rear spar. A young apprentice aircraft electrician was detailed to perform the operation. After removing the battery from its mounting, he balanced it on the top longeron prior to climbing out of the cabin. This was fatal! The battery toppled from its precarious perch and, with a crash which would have awakened the dead, disappeared into the immaculate centre section. It reappeared split-seconds later on the floor of the hangar amid sundry lengths of timber, ply and fabric! Jack Lavender, the Service Manager, failed to see the humorous side of the incident and it was rumoured that Bill Shakespear, after he had recovered from an epileptic fit, had to be restrained from doing physical injury to the youngster!

The Proctor and its many variants were used extensively by the Royal Navy and the Royal Air Force in many theatres of war and in spite of its shortcomings performed its duties of communications and radio training satisfactorily.

With the exception of the length which increased by six inches (25 ft 10

The radio installation in the
Proctor Mk III. In this
version the crew was reduced
to two. The footwell visible
in the centre section behind
the lower radio crate
accommodated the radio
operator in the Mk II version
(Royal Aircraft
Establishment).

in) the overall dimensions were identical to those of the Vega Gull. The empty weight had increased to 2,180 lb against the 1,740 lb of the Vega Gull but the all-up weight remained the same at 3,250 lb. The protuberances, such as the oil cooler and the generator cowling etc. had made inroads on the performance figures – even with the slightly lower power loading figure of 15.6 lb/hp and there had been a loss of 4 mph on the maximum speed which was down to 170 mph. The cruising speed had degenerated to 155 mph, some 15 mph slower than that of the Vega Gull.

From the experiences gained on the Proctor and its variants a new aircraft was designed to meet the Air Ministry specification T9/41 but some changes had taken place in the 'top management'. In 1940 Capt Percival had resigned his post as Managing Director and Chief Test Pilot, his former duties being taken over by Capt Peter D. Ackland, the latter by Capt L. T. Carruthers. On the design side, Arthur Bage, who had previously converted the out-line designs of Percival into practical flying machines, was appointed Chief Designer, able to practice his art with fewer constraints.

His first design under these new conditions was to meet the T9/41 specification, the name Preceptor being suggested but rejected in favour of retaining the existing class-name Proctor. Although the new aircraft bore a strong family resemblance to its predecessor it was, in fact, a totally new aeroplane and was therefore allocated the design letters 'Ae'. It was designed from the outset to be a dual-role machine; a three-seat radio trainer which could be quickly and easily converted to its second role, that of a communications aircraft with four seats and dual controls for use by the Royal Air Force and Royal Navy.

Although the same structural principles were employed for the wooden airframe, many detail changes and improvements were incorporated,

An export model, the Proctor IV supplied to the Lebanese (Charles Brown).

The radio installation in the Proctor IV. Note the levers at the top of the windscreen frame by which the doors could be jettisoned and the warning notice stencilled on the door (Sport and General).

particularly in the servicing and role versatility aspects. The same wing span was retained but the area was increased to 202 sq ft against the 197 sq ft of the earlier marks. The overall length increased to 28 ft 2 in and the height to 8 ft 4 in. With an all-up weight of 3,500 lb the wing loading was 17.3 lb/sq ft. The same power unit was used – the de Havilland Gipsy Queen Series II driving a constant-speed propeller – which gave a power loading of 16.8 lb/hp. The Proctor IV, as the aircraft had been named, being a slightly larger

The one-and-only Proctor VI powered by a Gipsy Queen 32 displays its identification feature − the floats.

The completed Proctor VI with fairings on the float support struts (Hugh Scanlan).

and heavier aeroplane, had a reduced top speed of 157 mph and a cruising speed of 140 mph. The stalling speed had increased to 55 mph with the flaps down.

To permit easy conversion to the communications role which required dual controls, the control column, rudder bar (adjustable for reach by means of a star-wheel), the seat and some ancillary equipment were mounted as an integral unit on an easily removable platform attached to brackets on the spar box of the centre section. To accommodate this, the depth of the fuselage was increased. The Proctor IV was easily identified by the large sliding windows in the rear of the cabin and the pre-formed curved decking on the underside of the fuselage. The moulded windscreen was also much deeper and the engine-driven generator housed within the cowlings which obviated the need for the unsightly blister as on its earlier sisters.

The tailplane was rigidly mounted on cast light alloy brackets bolted to the top longerons and both the elevator and the rudder were fitted with trim-tabs which were adjustable in flight by means of handwheels and gearboxes mounted on the ceiling of the cabin between the jettisonable doors.

When operating as a radio trainer a T/R1154/55 radio installation was

The wings of a Proctor IV are unfolded on the apron in front of the camouflaged Experimental Hangar. The silver painted aircraft on the left was a Proctor IV, NP336, specially prepared for the Duke of Gloucester.

79

mounted in a cradle alongside the pilot; the radio operator being provided with a foot-well in the spar-box of the centre section. The third member of the crew was accommodated in a single seat in the rear of the cabin. This could easily be removed and a bench seat installed when used in the communications role.

The aeroplane was 'right' from the start and if my memory serves me correctly, few – if any – modifications were needed to rectify faults. The type was destined to be the last wooden aeroplane to be designed and built by the company and only eight pre-production machines were built at Luton, the rest of the production run being constructed by F. Hills and Sons, furniture manufacturers, at their works in Trafford Park, Manchester.

Two special versions were constructed, one in 1944 designated the Proctor IVa with ply-covered wings and a generally strengthened airframe for use as a flying testbed for the de Havilland Gipsy Queen 50 & 70 engines and a seaplane for the Hudson's Bay Co. This was designated the Proctor VI and delivered to them in 1947. A metal version of the Proctor V, the civil version of the Proctor IV, was considered. This incorporated many refinements such as sliding doors to the cabin. The name Pewit was tentatively chosen to continue the company's tradition of naming their aircraft after members fo the gull species. However, as the considerable number of Proctor aircraft of all marks that were being released by the Royal Air Force and the Fleet Air Arm were satisfying the civil demand, the project was discontinued.

A number of Proctor Vs were purchased by the Lebanese and, not previously having an air force, asked the company to design the national markings. Being considered 'artistic', I was given this task. The tail markings, on the insistance of the liaising Colonel, included a symbolised Cedar tree which was their national emblem. When the finished aircraft was posted to the flight shed, some wag had pasted a drawing of a dog standing on three legs (and doing what dogs do in that position) at the base of the tree. On the rectification list the inspector instructed '. . . chase off dog and wash down tree'.

CHAPTER 6

THE YEARS OF HOSTILITY

During the dark years of the war, as one National Emergency passed so another took its place. When the Battle of Britain was in full spate and its duration was unknown to the Allied Command, Fighter Command considered the possibility of being faced with a shortage of fighter aircraft with which to meet the threat of the Luftwaffe now based in France and the Low Countries and within a short flying time of its targets in England. In response to this the Ministry of Aircraft Production, a body established under Lord Beaverbrook to direct and co-ordinate the Aircraft Industry, issued a specification for a fighter aeroplane which, to conserve the use of strategic materials (steel and light alloys), was to be of wooden construction. A Rolls-Royce Merlin XX power unit was specified and the design had to be reasonably simple to restrict the cost and improve the production.

In response to this, Arthur Bage produced a design based on the aerodynamic configuration of the Mew Gull but somewhat larger. In the event the contract was won by Miles Aircraft of Woodley, Reading, who built two prototype machines which were designated the M.20, the first flying nine weeks and two days after receiving the authority to proceed. When the design programme for the Proctor IV had been completed, the Drawing Office was busily engaged on modifications and repair schemes with a few other small projects thrown in for good measure. One of these was the refurbishing of the French designed and built Caudron Simoun, a low-wing, single engined cabin monoplane, a reasonable number having been flown into England by the Free French Forces. The repairs to the wooden structure presented little problem and damaged undercarriages could, fortunately, be replaced by those fitted to the Proctor. The major task was the replacement of the Bengali Six engine with the more readily available de Havilland Gipsy Six and Gipsy Queen power units.

One of these aeroplanes was delivered on a low-loader (colloquially known as a 'Queen Mary' due to its exceptional length) to serve as a trials installation and test aircraft. As an aside, it was my practice to inspect as many aircraft as possible to make sketches of interesting or novel devices for future reference. I was doing my customary tour of investigation on the Simoun when I spied a small cube attached to the instrument panel directly in front of the pilot's position. It was held at the bottom by a small lever. Having no idea as to what purpose the device served, I tentatively prodded the lever with my pencil. Immediately I was startled by a loud clatter and the long chain of small square plates that cascaded down in front of me! I had found the fire-warning indicator!

The re-design of the engine installation, allocated the design letters 'Ac',

Three views of the model of the huge wooden transport aeroplane proposed by Arthur Bage. The final design was powered by six Bristol Centaurus engines and the Burnelli-type fuselage provided a vast hold twelve feet in height. Troops would have been accommodated within the twin tail booms.

was managed by Harry Frankland, one of the Senior Design Draughtsmen. No modification was to be made to the engine management system which operated contrary to that used on British aeroplanes, i.e. the throttle was opened by pulling the lever. At the completion of the test programme it was arranged that Harry should accompany Capt Carruthers on a pre-delivery flight. Although many flights had previously been made without incident, on this occasion – the first with a passenger – Carruthers was probably distracted and, without thinking, pulled the throttle closed after he had taxied back to the apron. Immediately the tail of the Simoun rose and the

nose buried itself in turf, fortunately without serious damage.

A quantity of Curtis Sea Mew aircraft had been supplied under the Lease-Lend agreement and, to put it kindly, were redundant in their original role. They were not successful aeroplanes so it was decided by higher authorities that they could be usefully employed as radio-controlled target aircraft (or rather that was what we were told), the contract for the design and installation of the systems being awarded to Percivals. A Sea Mew was delivered (what a cumbersome brute it was) and a small team was deployed to undertake the work. After residing in the Service hangar for many months, during which much of the radio-control equipment was installed, the aircraft simply disappeared. Whether the job was completed or the aircraft successfully flown remains a complete mystery to me.

In 1943 when most of Europe was occupied by the Third Reich, the lines of communication to the Allied Forces in the Middle East were extremely over-extended. Most supplies were hazardously transported by sea. As a relatively small quantity of these essential supplies had been flown in, Arthur Bage reasoned that, as air transport had been proved feasible, a greater contribution could be made by using an aeroplane with a greater payload. To meet this criterion he designed a large transport aircraft based on the Burnelli Flying Wing principle.

It was envisaged that four (eventually six) Bristol Centaurus engines would power the wooden monster, wood having been selected as it was a non-strategic material. The aerofoil body (it could hardly be termed a fuselage) was somewhat deeper in section than the wings and provided a hold of vast volume some twelve feet in height and entered via a ramp in the underside. Troops were to be accommodated in the twin booms which carried the tailplane (on the outer sides of the booms and interconnected by a strut), the twin fins and rudders. The crew was to have been housed in a cabin protruding from the leading edge of the body.

Two power units were to be mounted at the wing junction and the remaining engines on the leading edges of the mainplanes. The main units of the tricycle undercarriage, each fitted with two wheels, retracted upwards and forwards while the nose unit retracted sideways.

A model of the proposed aeroplane fitted with four engines was built but, in spite of much lobbying which even included an article published in the February issue of the *Aeroplane*, nothing became of the project.

To meet the demands for a twin-engined training aircraft, a contract was awarded to the company for the construction and assembly of Airspeed Oxfords, of which some 1,300 were built at the rate of between thirty and forty a week. This was no mean feat with a total labour force of less than 2,000 employees! It was during this period that the company suffered a major set-back to its production when the Embodiment Loan Stores caught light during the early hours of the morning. Although the conflagration was confined to the stores area, a fair amount of damage was caused by the enthusiastic firemen who, to save the almost completed aircraft, pushed them away from the seat of the fire. Unfortunately all were on jacks and

During the war the company built Airspeed Oxford and DH Mosquito aircraft under sub-contract. Here ten Mosquitos, the product of a week's labour, await delivery (Charles E. Brown).

trestles which passed through the wings.

New aircraft were leaving the production line at a spanking pace and to assist the hard-pressed company pilots, a number of serving officers of the Royal Air Force were seconded by the company – and what a grand bunch they were! One of them, F/O Russell was a most likeable character who before the war had participated in the RAF Pageants at Hendon flying Hawker Furies. He had been badly crippled as a result of polio, but through sheer determination had convinced the Medical Board that he was fit to fly again.

He was also convinced that he would never lose his life in a flying accident but unfortunately he was wrong. It was Russell's habit, after completing the test programme, to set the Oxford on a heading for home and, after trimming the machine, leave the pilot's seat to join his passengers in the cabin for a chat, reassuring them that ''. . . as we are the biggest aircraft flying in this area, the smaller fry will have to get out of our way!''

He eventually lost his life when the Proctor in which he was flying crashed near Edlesborough, although his passenger, 'Snowy' Joiner – one of the ground engineers – survived. During the subsequent investigation as to the cause of the crash, it was found that the 'Perspex' cover over the landing light had collapsed which caused the wing to disintegrate through air pressure. Throughout the entire wartime test flying programme this was the only fatility to be suffered by the company.

A rather amusing incident was related by Jack Short, one of the AID Inspectors. The tale revolved around a Polish pilot of the ATA and Jack, being a past-master at story telling, unfolded it imitating the broken English used by that gentleman. Soon after taking off the pilot returned to base with several holes cut roughly in the wall of the Oxford's fuselage. The Pole explained that soon after becoming airborne the undercarriage position indicator lamps had failed and, unable to see the starboard undercarriage leg from his position, had cut the holes with his 'leetle' penknife. ". . . I make ze 'ole, I no see, I make 'nudder 'ole. I see d' untercarriage. It is down . . . I land! You fix eh?'

Following the Oxfords, the company undertook the construction and assembly of the de Havilland Mosquito, of which some 245 were made before the contract was cancelled when the war ended. The test flight of the first Mosquito built at Luton was undertaken by Capt Carruthers but, although the actual flight was uneventful, when preparing to land it was found that the tail wheel refused to come down. In spite of using all known techniques, Carruthers was forced to land with the tail wheel still retracted. He made a perfect 'two-wheeler' and by the judicious use of the brakes and engines, kept the tail up until the forward speed had decayed to a minimum. When the tail finally dropped, hardly any damage was caused.

For many decades aircraft used for *ab initio* training had been relatively simple and although the Tiger Moths and Magisters on which most pilots had received their basic training were excellent aircraft, they were somewhat out of date for teaching the new techniques of flying which, by that time, was entering the jet age; thus, toward the end of hostilities, the company began work on its first metal aeroplane . . . but that is a different story to be told in the next chapter.

Prentice T.Mk 1, VR227, displays the final empennage configuration which finally overcame the spinning problems. The generous wing area is also apparent (Percival Aircraft Ltd.)

CHAPTER 7
THE PRENTICE

During the war British flying training schools had been established in many parts of the world and from these a vast amount of information had been collated on all aspects of pilot training which, when analysed, was to have a remarkable effect in later years. The analysis revealed that considerable costs had been expended on elementary training given on simple, relatively easy to fly aeroplanes, but had been wasted when the novice pilot, confronted with the complexities of more advanced aircraft with controllable propellers and comprehensive instrumentation, was unable to make the transition.

Furthermore, the psychological effect of being rejected for further pilot training after achieving solo flight and apparently well on the way to gaining the coveted 'wings' could be most traumatic and possibly effect re-mustering into another branch of the service. To eliminate this, it was proposed that *ab initio* training should be given on aircraft equipped with the refinements of their more advanced counterparts. By adopting this principle, it was argued, the inability of the embryo pilot to comprehend the complexities of modern flight would be revealed at an early stage, thus saving valuable resources and expenditure.

To conform to this, specification T23/43 was issued. It decreed that the *ab initio* training aeroplane should be capable of all-weather flying, be fully aerobatic and carry full radio equipment. Furthermore, for economy, a third seat was to be provided to give embryo pilots air experience. The power unit specified was a development of the well-proven D.H. Gipsy Six engine. In all it was a very difficult specification to meet.

The design proposals submitted by the company were accepted and in late 1944 work started under the design letters 'Aj' on what was eventually to be known as the Prentice. The incompatible design parameters resulted in an unusually robust airframe with a mass of equipment unknown on previous *ab initio* trainers, all hauled around the sky by a DH Gipsy Queen 32 engine of 250 hp driving a constant-speed propeller.

The introduction of metal for aircraft production brought about many changes in the workshops. With wooden structures the need for jigs was minimal; a totally different story when metal was used. Massive structures based on RSJs sprang up over the shop floor in which the various components were assembled and, to reduce the time needed to produce the frames and ribs, a large 'rubber press' was installed.

The term 'rubber press' stemmed from the method employed. In this only a male die manufactured from an extremely hard wood-based material called 'Jabroc', which was resistant to the high compression forces of the press, was required. A flat outline of the rib or former was placed over the

The prototype Prentice T.Mk I in its original form with the typical Percival outline to the fin and rudder. The large wing and canopy created considerable disturbance in the airflow over the empennage which resulted in abysmal spinning qualities (Flight).

die and located in position by metal dowels. This was then covered by a thick blanket of very hard rubber and inserted in the press. A high pressure was then applied which forced the unsupported area of the metal downwards. Such a method could be used effectively on light alloys and thus obviated the need for the expensive male and female dies required in the forming of steel sheet.

At about the same time lofting (accurately drawing the various items full size on metal sheets) was introduced, the 'Lofting Floor' being under the control of T. Harold Nightingale, a brilliant mathematician who had been 'directed' into the company at the beginning of the war from his peace-time occupation in the insurance industry, the move being most advantageous to the company.

In conjunction with Christopher Burt, the Chief Photographer, he developed a system whereby the lofting sheets could be accurately duplicated; the copies being used directly as templates, thus obviating errors and speeding the production of templates considerably. A special laboratory was built in the Photographic Department with large vertical tanks sunk into the floor. An overhead gantry and mobile hoist was installed to handle the large sheets. The original loft sheets were mounted on a vacuum easel and photographed on to large glass negatives. These were then used to project an image on to aluminium or duraluminium sheets which had been coated with a diazo solution sensitive to ultra-violet light. As far as can be established this was the first time such a system had been used.

The fuselage was constructed in two portions, the front half being the 4 ft 2 in wide cabin. The sides and bottom were built as semi-braced structures with light alloy skinning. A strong girder box was built into the bottom half of this assembly to which the wings were bolted. The rear half of the fuselage was a semi-monocoque structure of light alloy frames and stringers covered by a skin of light alloy.

The student and his instructor sat side-by-side under an enormous canopy with the third member of the crew in glorious isolation in a vast cockpit at the rear. Access to the front seats was through large independently-sliding and jettisonable doors, and the rear seat through an up-and-over sliding door on the port side which was dubbed 'the fish fryer' by the design staff.

The two-part cantilever wing with a liberal area of 305 sq ft (nearly twice as much as the Gull) was built on two spars with a false-spar to dissipate the loads imposed by the ailerons and flaps. Full-depth ribs were situated between the spars at approximately 20 in pitch with three former-ribs equally spaced between them on the top and bottom surfaces. The complete structure was covered by a skin of light alloy. The fabric-covered ailerons had 'D' section spars at their leading edges and pressed light alloy ribs. The starboard aileron was fitted with a trim tab which was adjustable on the ground only.

The pneumatically-operated split trailing edge flaps between the

The instrument panel of the Prentice T.Mk 1, this particular example being destined for Argentina. The missing instrument was the clock which, being 'valuable and attractive', was not fitted until the last moment (Harold Cox).

89

The split trailing edge flaps were of generous area and extended from aileron to aileron. A device was fitted to prevent a rapid retraction as their immediate retraction would have caused the aircraft to sink (Percival Aircraft Ltd).

ailerons and including the fuselage were built in three sections and of generous area. In the event of a baulked landing the immediate retraction of these huge areas would have caused the aircraft to sink. To prevent this a safety device was fitted. During the early flights it was found that, with the undercarriage legs reaching almost full compression at touch-down, the ground clearance with the flaps fully extended was perilously limited, so, to increase this, the chord was reduced by some four inches over the middle 70% of their span.

The empennage was an all-metal cantilever structure, the tailplane comprising two spars, pressed ribs and light alloy skinning. It was rigidly bolted to cast-alloy brackets mounted on the rear fuselage. The fabric-covered rudder and the elevators were similar in construction to the ailerons and were fitted with trimming tabs which were adjustable in flight through manually-operated gearboxes mounted on the wall of the cabin for the pilot and on the centre line for the instructor. All flying controls were cable operated and particular attention was given to the reduction of friction, pulleys fitted with ball-races being used at the changes of direction.

A fixed divided type undercarriage with a track of 12 ft gave excellent ground stability and was mounted in castings bolted to the front spar of the wing; the fairings being similar to those fitted to the previous designs – the Gull, Vega Gull and Proctor. Pneumatically-operated brakes were fitted to the wheels and were applied by a lever on the control column with differential application controlled by the rudder bar. A fully castoring and self-centring tailwheel was bolted to the stern post.

The engine (a de Havilland Gipsy Queen 32) was mounted on triangulated steel-tube bearers bolted to the front of the fuselage and were enclosed by a four-panel cowling, the side panels hinging at the top centre line. The power unit was mounted quite low in the airframe and this, coupled with the high seating position of the flying crew, gave a remarkably unobstructed view to the pilots.

Fuel was carried in two crash-proof tanks mounted in the wing roots between the spars. An oil tank of 4.9 gallon capacity, fitted with a device which prevented lubricant starvation when the aircraft was inverted, was

mounted in the leading edge of the port wing with an oil cooler mounted on its inboard side, the cooling air entering through an aperture in the leading edge.

To give the student pilot night flying experience a new simulated system was adopted. In this, amber-coloured screens were fitted to the cockpit windows and, when under night flying instruction, the pupil wore blue-tinted goggles. This, in effect, cut off all visual contact with the world outside except for the sodium approach lights of the airfield; these remained clearly visible although, within the cockpit, everything could be seen – albeit through a blue tint. The instructor, on the other hand, retained total visibility, the amber side screens could be slid backwards and the panels over the windscreen folded and lowered in channels when not required.

The maiden flight of the Prentice was made by Capt L. T. Carruthers on 31 March 1946. During the early flights lateral instability became apparent when, without warning, the aircraft flipped over on to its back during a gentle turn. To improve stability the effective dihedral was increased by 2° 25′ to a total of 6° by turning the tips of the wings up at an angle of 30°.

A number of Prentice aircraft were supplied to foreign Governments. These on the production line at Luton were destined for the Argentine Air Force (Percival Aircraft Ltd).

During the spinning trials an anti-spin parachute was mounted on top of the fuselage aft of the canopy and a guard erected over the rudder horn-balance (Flight).

The spinning characteristics were also most unsatisfactory and to improve them the rudder area was increased, destroying the classic Percival outline, and anti-spin strakes were fitted. This made little difference.

During the initial design stages Arthur Bage had opted for simplicity, employing uncomplicated split trailing-edge flaps on wings of generous area, whereas the Assistant Chief Designer, R. F. 'Bruvver' Davies (the nickname stemming from his habit of calling all-and-sundry 'Bruvver') advocated a smaller wing fitted with complex Gouge-type flaps to achieve the same ends, maintaining that once the large wing started spinning it would be difficult to stop. In the event he was proved right, as most, if not all the difficulties experienced were with spinning.

After two or three turns the spin would rapidly become flat and the subsequent recovery both prolonged and difficult, if not impossible without the use of the anti-spinning parachute stowed in a box mounted on the top of the fuselage just forward of the fin. A full-blooded investigation was mounted to correct this most serious fault.

The traditional Percival-shaped fin was the first thing to be sacrificed in the ensuing spate of modifications. Many empennage configurations were explored, including twin fins and rudders, and the tailplane shot up and down the fin at a speed which would have done credit to an express lift in the Empire State Building! Even the length of the fuselage was increased, which was a rather drastic piece of surgery. The shape and area of the elevators was progressively changed and at one stage they were mounted beyond the tailplane on a torque-tube rather like the Pearson rotary aileron – but at the back! This proved to be the most effective solution, so a compromise was made which resulted in the unsightly elevator profile finally employed.

There were some very tense moments during the flight trials and in one incident, after successfully completing the preliminary short spins, the pilot climbed to regain the height lost. With the power available this took quite a few minutes. After about five minutes had elapsed the note of the engine dropped and the nose began to rise as the stall was approached, the wing dropped and the Prentice began its slow gyration toward mother earth in the dreaded prolonged spin.

After a few turns the spin flattened but the rotation continued as the pilot conducted his corrective measures – but with little effect. After what to us on the ground seemed hours, the pilot streamed his drag-chute to regain control. Although no longer flat the spin continued until the machine was perilously close to the ground where the spectators, unheard by the pilot, were imploring him to bale out. At the last minute control was regained and the pilot landed from the final dive with the drag-chute still streamed. On inspection it was found that the guard erected over the rudder horn had collapsed and had allowed the drag-chute to pass between the fin and rudder; the shroud lines had then restricted rudder movement.

Many tail configurations were used experimentally to overcome the abysmal spinning qualities of the Prentice (Percival Aircraft Ltd).

The Prentice T.Mk 1 tended to flatten after two or three turns of a spin. Twin fins and rudders were fitted in an attempt to rectify the fault (Percival Aircraft Ltd).

When compared with its *ab-initio* predecessors the Prentice was certainly a hefty beast, having a wing span of 46 ft, a length of 31 ft 3 in, and an overall height of 12 ft 10½ in. It was also exceedingly strong – the test specimen withstood loads in excess of 10 g – and in spite of an all-up weight of 3,790 lb (which gave a wing loading of 12.421 lb/sq ft, and a power loading of 15.1 lb/hp), the performance was quite acceptable, with a maximum speed of 143 mph. It cruised at 134 mph and had a stalling speed of 56.6 mph. With standard tanks providing a total capacity of 40 gallons, the range was 396 miles.

One of my many tasks at that time was the preparation of procedures to be followed during servicing. One of these was the removal of the fuel tank situated between the spars in the root of the wing, inboard of the under carriage. The tank was accessible through a panel secured by dozens of screws. We assessed the task with the aircraft resting on its undercarriage and found that there was ample ground clearance for the tank to clear the structure. Without further ado the panel was removed and we proceeded to make our notes and sketches. But when we came to replace the panel we found, to our horror, that it did not fit! The aperture had changed shape. The loads on the undercarriage legs – which were almost 20° off the vertical, had distorted the wing! The aircraft was quickly placed on jacks and trestles in the rigging position and, thankfully, everything returned to normal.

Six prototypes were ordered, one of which was used as a structural test specimen, but the first flying example carried the serial number TV163 These were followed by six pre-production aircraft, the first, VN684, being delivered to the Empire Flying School at Hullavington on 27 August 1947 to

undertake Service evaluation trials and the compilation of the pilot's notes, the latter being done by the Handling Squadron at Mamby. The Prentice did not, however, officially enter Royal Air Force service until 1 October of the same year.

Dick Wheldon – who became the company's Chief Pilot – prepares to fly a production version of the Prentice T.Mk 1.

As was usual, the first unit to be equipped with the Prentice was the Central Flying School who took delivery of their new aircraft on 30 July 1948 and based them at the satellite station of South Cerney where they were used by instructors to formulate the training procedures. By this time the third seat, considered by the policymakers to be so important when they prepared the specification, was no longer used. Needless to say, it was not long before the instructors were demonstrating their prowess with their new mounts, their piece de resistance being a display of close formation aerobatics in three machines linked together by strips of webbing 12 ft long, the display culminating, despite the low reserve of power, in a loop. An average of 750 instructors per annum on courses of 16 weeks duration were trained on the Prentice.

The next unit to receive its full allocation of 30 aeroplanes was the elite Royal Air Force College at Cranwell, their first machine, VR243, arriving on 3 August 1948. By 15 September sufficient aircraft had been delivered to enable the exclusive training of cadets on the Prentice to begin and the first fully trained officer cadets, the No. 46 entry, passed out on 8 April 1949.

No. 3 Flying Training School (FTS), then based at Feltwell, was the next

Bearing the temporary civil registration G-AKLF, an extensive tour was made in company with G-AKLG which resulted in a number of export orders.

to be equipped, their aeroplanes being delivered fifteen days after Cranwell had received theirs. This was quickly followed by the delivery of VS261 and VS263 on 1 September to No. 6 FTS at Ternhill. In the following year more units were re-equipped. The first was No. 7 FTS based at Cottesmore, followed by No. 22 at Syerston and finally No. 2 FTS at Hullavington in February, March and June respectively, the rate of the re-equipment being possible due to the large stock which had built up at the maintenance units.

Eventually the Royal Air Force received 400 examples of the type of which 75 were built under sub-contract by Blackburn Aircraft Ltd, and it is interesting to note that during the interchangeability tests on the two products, although the engine cowlings of the aeroplanes built by Percivals would fit those constructed by Blackburns, the reverse was not possible.

Two early production machines, temporarily registered G-AKLG and 'KLF with an overall livery of yellow with black lettering and the legend 'Percival Prentice' inscribed in English (which was changed to Greek during the tour) and Arabic on the engine cowlings, undertook an extended sales tour with WgCdr A. N. Kingwill and the chief test pilot R. G. (Dickie) Wheldon as the pilots. From this tour a number of export sales were secured, the Argentine Air Force ordering 100 machines, the Lebanese three and the Indian Air Force twenty, with a further 42 which were to be built under licence by Hindustan Aeronautics. The first machine to be built by this establishment was flown on 30 April 1949 in the hands of Capt Murishi.

As an alternative power unit a supercharged de Havilland Gipsy Queen 51 engine of 296 hp was fitted, and with this the aircraft was designated the Prentice T Mk.2. (The first aeroplanes were designated Prentice T.Mk.1.) There was no increase in the overall dimensions but the maximum speed increased to 156 mph, which was an improvement of 13 mph, but only the prototype was built. A further derivation, known as the Prentice T.Mk.3, powered by a Gipsy Queen 71 supercharged engine of 345 hp driving a

three-bladed constant-speed propeller was built which gave the aircraft a maximum speed of 171 mph. My records show that this aeroplane was used by the de Havilland Engine Company as a flying test-bed, whereas other authoritative publications state that it was delivered to the Indian Air Force.

After a relatively short service life of six years (short when compared with that of over a quarter of a century enjoyed by its ultimate successor the Jet Provost) the Prentice was gradually withdrawn, its demise being hastened by the introduction of the superior Provost T Mk.1. The disposal began in the December of 1953 with many of the earlier products being scrapped, although a number were used as maintenance airframes.

The sole example of the Prentice T.Mk 3 was powered by a DH Gipsy Queen 71 supercharged engine of 345 hp (Percival Aircraft Ltd).

Aviation Traders Ltd purchased 252 redundant Prentices which were intended to be converted for the civil market but only 25 were sold. G-APJB, photographed at Sywell in July 1975, was modified to accommodate five people (Air Portraits).

Aviation Traders (Engineering) Ltd of Southend headed by that entrepreneur (Sir) Freddie Laker – later of 'Sky Train' fame – made history by purchasing 252 of the redundant aircraft which, it was intended, were to be offered on the civil market as glider-tugs, banner towing aircraft, ambulance aircraft, crop sprayers and aerial limousines. In spite of the low price – £1,400 to £2,000 dependent upon the standard of modification – only 25 were sold, the project being killed by the high operating costs caused by the thirsty engine and the lifting of the importation ban on lighter and much more efficient American aircraft.

Perhaps the most well known civil Prentice was G-AOKH, used by BMK/Lambtex Rugs Ltd as a banner towing aircraft to advertise their products until banned by Government order. By December 1975 only nine Prentices remained in an airworthy condition and one static example is preserved by the Newark Air Museum.

In 1944 Percival Aircraft Ltd was acquired by the Hunting Group of Companies and W. A. (Bill) Summers, who had resigned before the outbreak of the war, returned as managing director. He replaced Capt Peter Ackland who had run the outfit since the resignation of Capt E. W. Percival. Under the new management the letter identification of the projects was dropped in favour of numbers prefixed by the letter 'P', thus the Prentice became the P40, and the Proctor V, although an earlier product but still being built when the Hunting Group took over, took the later P44 project number.

In a fit of enthusiasm the Sales Manager, Y. Galitzine (a White Russian Prince), allocated 'P' numbers to all previous designs – from the Gull onwards and including all 'paper aeroplanes', but this was purely a cosmetic exercise designed to convert historical facts into the methodical systems of the Hunting Group.

CHAPTER 8

THE MERGANSER AND PRINCE

For almost five years I had worked for Percival Aircraft Ltd, the last five in the dual roles of draughtsman and technical illustrator, the latter title being somewhat of a misnomer. At that time the publications department was quite a small outfit with a total staff of four. If necessary, and if one had the ability, any job had to be undertaken. As a result I became a technical author, a schedule compiler and even a typist − in addition to my primary roles of draughtsman and technical illustrator!

Under these conditions and finding publications work more to my taste, in 1944 I obtained a post in the publications department of the de Havilland Aircraft Company where I worked on the documentation for the Mosquito F.33 (I think) on which the wings folded, the operation being carried out manually by means of a large baulk of timber which slotted into pegs on the underside of the wing. I also undertook some work on the Vampire.

It is strange how a conversation can be misconstrued if only one side is heard. This happened when Mr Westlake-James, who was Head of the department, was discussing the effects of flying for a long duration in a pressurised cockpit. The conversation was by telephone and all we in the office heard was . . . ''Yes, Squadron Leader . . . I know the pressure becomes unbearable when you have been flying for a long time . . . but you do have a cock to relieve yourself . . .'' One of the demure tracers disgraced herself by giggling uncontrollably!

Although the staff at de Havillands were a grand crew − David Kossoff and Sq Ldr A. H. Curtiss among them − the remoteness of the individual in such a large organisation was not to my liking; therefore, when I was invited to rejoin my old company I did so at the earliest opportunity.

On returning after an absence of one year the company was busily engaged in the production and conversion of the Proctor for the civil market. The first Prentices were on the production line and the Merganser, designed to meet the need for small feeder-line aircraft had flown. The flight shed, having spare capacity, was servicing the Avro Ansons of Hunting Air Travel and a variety of aeroplanes used by the Luton Flying Club which had also been resurrected by the Hunting Group. Several other aircraft were being serviced under contract, one being a gleaming twin-engined Beech 18 that always seemed to have a team constantly polishing it, consuming tons of 'Duraglit' in the process, and a de Havilland Dominie owned by Billy Butlin of holiday camp fame.

Another interesting aircraft that arrived from the United States of America in a packing case was a Globe Swift. Assembled by the staff of the service hangar, it was a diminutive two-seat low-wing monoplane of all-

metal construction with an electrically-operated retractable undercarriage. The stressed-skin principle was taken to the nth degree and the absence of internal structure (each wing panel had a spar and four main ribs; the fuselage four frames) made the aircraft appear to be most flimsy in comparison with the massive structures of the Prentice and Merganser.

The Merganser, allocated the design letters 'Au' before the introduction of its P48 designation, had the doubtful distinction of being the only fixed-wing aeroplane (apart from the ER.189 D which was purely a research aircraft) not to enter production. To keep costs within reasonable bounds, many of the components used on the Prentice were embodied in its design, the flying surfaces – suitably modified – being a major contribution. The empennage units were those originally designed for the Prentice before the extensive modification needed to rectify that aeroplane's abysmal spinning qualities.

The fuselage, which accommodated a crew of two with five passengers in a spacious, sound-proofed cabin 15 ft long by 5 ft 6 in wide and 6 ft in height, was the only major new component. The cabin was entered through a door 2 ft wide by 5 ft high at the rear and on the port side. When used in the freighting role an adjacent door could be unlocked which increased the aperture to 5 ft in width, making the loading of bulky items an easy operation. The close proximity of the door-sill to the ground obviated the need for specialised handling equipment.

Immediately opposite the entrance door was the toilet compartment and if this was omitted a sixth passenger could be accommodated. At the front of the cabin, immediately aft of the crew's compartment, was a 110 cubic ft compartment for 300 lb of luggage which was accessible through a counter-balanced door 3 ft wide by 4 ft high, also in the port side. Without this compartment the complement of passengers could be increased to eight plus the crew of two. Overhead racks were provided for personal luggage and when used as a freighter with all internal equipment removed, the freight was lashed to special flush-fitting strong-points built into the floor structure.

The crew compartment, its floor being above the level of that in the cabin, was entered through a door in the bulkhead which separated the two

compartments. Access to the rear of the instrument panel, the flying and engine controls was through a hinged nose-cap. The crew members were in side-by-side seating protected by a deep 'V' shaped windscreen of flat safety-glass. Immediately in front of the crew was the instrument panel through which protruded the control 'columns'. These slid in the fore-and-aft plane to provide elevator movement, the ailerons being controlled by 'rams-horns' attached to them. Between the seats was a control pedestal that mounted the engine and airframe management levers.

Structurally, with suitable modifications, the Merganser was identical to the Prentice with the exception of the fuselage. This was built in three sections with joints at the rear of the crew compartment and the rear of the cabin. The structure comprised light alloy frames and stringers covered by a metal skin which was flush-riveted in the drag-sensitive areas with additional skinning riveted to the inner surfaces over the highly-stressed areas. Two longitudinal beams were built into the bottom of the nose section to dissipate the loads imposed by the non-steerable nose-wheel and to form a bay into which the unit retracted.

The wing attachment points were built into the top of the fuselage, the frames being reinforced to accept the loads imposed by the cantilever wings. On the wings (which had split trailing-edge flaps between the ailerons and fuselage but divided by the engine nacelles) were mounted two de Havilland Gipsy Queen 51 air-cooled engines, each of 296 hp. They were mounted as 'power eggs' on shock-proof light alloy bearers attached at six points. Each engine drove a de Havilland constant-speed and fully feathering three-bladed propeller.

The Merganser on Luton Airport before painting. Due to the non-availability of the Gipsy Queen 51 engines the aircraft was not put into production (Hayward Smeed & Co).

101

The ungainly vertical windscreen is most notable in this shot of the prototype Prince, G-ALCM (Flight).

Crash-proof fuel tanks with a total capacity of 105 gallons were mounted between the spars, inboard and outboard of each engine nacelle; the oil tanks (each with a capacity of 5 gallons) and the oil coolers were an integral part of the 'power egg'.

The mainwheel units of the tricycle undercarriage, fitted with medium pressure tyres, retracted backwards into the nacelles, a cast link at the top swung forward to reduce the length of the leg. When the landing gear was retracted all apertures were closed by doors, but these remained open when the gear was extended. It was the consensus of opinion among the 'top brass' of aeronautical engineering that pneumatics were unsuitable for undercarriage retraction, but Arthur Bage, with a lot of experience on the Prentice behind him, considered that the additional weight imposed by the hydraulic fluid and the necessary return pipes could not be justified and opted for the much simpler pneumatic system. In practice it was most successful.

The Merganser had a wing span of 47 ft 9 in, a length of 39 ft 8 in and a height over the rudder of 13 ft 9 in. The gross wing area of 319 sq ft gave a wing loading of 21 lb/sq ft. The power loading was 11.35 lb/hp. The aircraft had a maximum speed of 193 mph, a cruising speed of 183 mph and with the flaps and landing gear extended, stalled at 69 mph.

The fuselage was completed in November 1946 and was despatched overland to be exhibited at the Paris Aero Show, but the machine did not fly until mid 1947. Delays were experienced in the supply of the Gipsy Queen 51 engines which were being developed under Ministry finance, but eventually two units were loaned by the Ministry of Supply and this enabled the flight test programme to be undertaken. Due to the non-availability of the engines the company had no other option but to discontinue the P48 project but, nevertheless it served a useful purpose by providing a wealth of data which speeded the design and development of the larger and very successful Prince and all its variants.

Although I did not witness it, the first flight of the Merganser was undertaken by Capt L. T. Carruthers on 9 May 1947 and, by all accounts, was quite a traumatic event! After a series of high-speed taxying runs, Carruthers took off, but instead of making a circuit as planned, the aeroplane disappeared in a straight line toward Hitchin and at a low altitude. After a while the Merganser was seen approaching from the opposite direction from where it made a safe landing. It seemed that Carruthers, shortly after taking off, had found it almost impossible to move the controls to apply elevator and aileron movement simultaneously, which forced him to fly straight and level until he had sorted out the problem. It was found that a tortional wind-up of the push-pull control 'column' aggravated by fibre bearing-blocks had caused the trouble. This was soon rectified by substituting roller bearings for the offending blocks.

During the extensive flight trials it was found necessary to increase the fin area. It was then given an overall livery of metallic Royal Blue cellulose wih the registration G-AMAH (until then it had been flying under the class B marking X-2) in pale cream lettering with cheat-lines along the fuselage and engine cowlings. In this guise the aircraft was exhibited at the SBAC show held at Radlett in September 1947. For almost a year the Merganser continued to howl its way across the green turf of Luton Airport, seeming to make use of the depression at its centre to become airborne, to amass a wealth of data which was to be invaluable in the design and development of

The first production Prince, G-ALFZ, fitted with undercarriage doors which remained closed when the gear was extended (Percival Aircraft Ltd).

The cabin door of the Prince was divided and, when the central pillar was removed, quite large items such as a Leonides engine on its stillage could be loaded with ease (Percival Aircraft Ltd).

its bigger sister the Prince. The Merganser was finally withdrawn from use and dismantled in August 1948, the fuselage being acquired by a local chicken farmer to become the most expensive and luxurious hen-house ever built!

Eventually known as the Prince, the P50, although bearing a strong family resemblance to its precursor the Merganser, was an entirely new aeroplane, but retained the same aerodynamic configuration. It was a much larger and heavier machine with a wing span of 56 ft, a length of 42 ft 10 in and a height over the rudder of 16 ft 1 in. It was powered by two Alvis Leonides air-cooled nine-cylinder radial engines of 520 hp each, driving de Havilland three-bladed constant-speed, fully feathering and reversable propellers.

The crew's compartment and the cabin were identical in size and layout to that of the Merganser but the luggage compartment was moved to a position aft of the cabin area and was accessible through a door in the rear bulkhead. This rearrangement enabled a complement of eight passengers (plus the crew of two) to be normally carried. The forward luggage door was no longer fitted and two escape hatches were built into the top of the fuselage to replace the single hatch of the Merganser which was located in the last-but-one window in the starboard side.

Many versions were offered, the Mk I being the standard eight passenger layout fitted with a fully equipped toilet compartment and provision for 400 lb of luggage. A smaller toilet compartment was fitted to the Mk IA which permitted the fitting of a double seat at the rear of the cabin. This increased the passenger accommodation to ten. An executive version, the Mk IB, could be supplied with various seating arrangements, usually six with a drop-leaf table across the full width of the cabin between the two sets of facing seats with a well appointed toilet compartment and cloakroom at the rear. For short-haul operations a twelve passenger version fitted with lightweight seats at a reduced pitch was offered.

The fuselage was built in two sections, one comprising the crew compartment, the other the cabin and the rear portion. Both were of light alloy construction employing vertical frames, stringers and channel-members in areas of high stress concentration, the whole being covered by a skin of alclad sheet. A majority of the frames were recessed to allow the stringers to be continuous members. A secondary skin was riveted over highly stressed areas on the inner surfaces, and double frames were positioned at the wing attachment stations, the frames at the front spar location incorporating a strong load-carrying beam.

The well sound-proofed cabin had nine windows, four to port and five on the starboard side, all double glazed with a silica-gel container to prevent them steaming up. Flush-fitting seat pick-up points were built into the floor

The second production Prince – G-ALJA – made a tour to Bombay via the Near East and was flown under simulated airline conditions.

When the first production Prince was sold to Aeronorte, the aircraft was up-graded to Mk 2 standard with accommodation for ten passengers. It was damaged beyond economical repair in March 1952 (Percival Aircraft Ltd).

structure and these also served as freight-lashing points. The upholstered ceiling panels were hinged and could be easily unlocked to gain access to the flying controls, the pneumatic piping and ancillary services located in the top of the fuselage.

The mainplanes, bolted directly to the fuselage at three points, were of two-spar construction, the rear spar (in effect a subsidiary spar) dissipated the loads imposed by the ailerons and the NACA slotted flaps situated between the ailerons and fuselage but divided by the engine nacelles. Between the spars were full-depth ribs interspersed by former-ribs with span-wise stringers of 'top-hat' section. The entire assembly was covered by a skin of light alloy. The leading edge was constructed as a separate unit and riveted to flanges on the front spar.

The ailerons had 'D' section spars to which were riveted a small number of strategically placed riblets, the whole assembly being covered by a skin of light alloy, fluted to increase rigidity. (The ailerons of the Merganser were of metal construction but fabric-covered.) The flaps were of similar construction but were reinforced by stringers running span-wise and were covered by a smooth metal skin. An in-flight adjustable trim tab was fitted to the port aileron only.

The main structural members of the engine nacelles attached to the undersurface of the wing supported the engine mounting and the undercarriage attachments, the loads being dissipated through strong diagonal bulkheads between the spars of the wing. The triangular bay formed by these bulkheads housed the oil tanks and the flexible fuel tanks with a total capacity of 106 gallons were contained within the wing structure, inboard of the engines, in lined bays. Provision was made for two further fuel tanks, one in each wing outboard of the engine nacelles, which increased the fuel capacity to 173 gallons. Most, if not all, the Princes built had inboard and outboard tanks fitted as standard equipment.

The single-piece tailplane was constructed with a main spar positioned just forward of the elevator shroud, a leading edge spar and a short auxiliary spar extending to the second rib on each side of the centre line. The ribs were recessed to accommodate the continuous stringers which ran from tip-

The instrument layout of the Prince showing the 'push-pull' control columns. The brake lever has yet to be fitted to the right-hand control yoke (Percival Aircraft Ltd).

A variety of seating arrangements were offered in the capacious cabin of the Prince from the high-density 12 seater to the six seat executive version shown here (Hunting Percival Aircraft Ltd).

to-tip, and the whole assembly was covered by a stressed metal skin. The two elevators, both fitted with trim tabs which were adjustable in flight, consisted of a main spar, an auxiliary spar and chordwise ribs covered by a skin of fluted light alloy, unlike those fitted to the Merganser which were fabric covered. The elevators were identical in construction and were interchangeable.

The fin comprised a post built of angle-section booms, their lower halves doubled for reinforcement, riveted to a flat web with flanged ribs extending forward to the leading edge. The structure was covered by a light alloy skin. The horn-balanced rudder was similar in construction to the elevators. A fluid de-icing system was installed in the leading edges of all flying surfaces.

A tricycle type undercarriage with a two-wheeled non-steerable nose unit and single-wheeled main units were fitted. Oleo-pneumatic suspension was used and the undercarriage doors remained closed except when the landing gear was retracted or extended. The main undercarriage compression leg was attached to forged brackets bolted to the strong diagonal ribs

108

between the spars of the wing via a forged pivoting link and was braced by a 'V' strut of steel tubes running forward and upward to forged brackets bolted to the nacelle bulkhead immediately behind the engine installation. The pivoting link was connected by two struts and a yoke to a further bracket toward the top centre of the bulkhead. A pneumatic retraction ram was fitted between the yoke and the 'V' strut.

During retraction the ram moved the 'V' strut upward and the yoke downward the latter swinging the pivoting link (through the two struts) forward and upward. The top of the compression leg, being attached to it, moved in the same direction. The 'V' strut, which was of a fixed length, restrained this forward movement and converted it into a rearward and upward one at the wheel. Although this narrative tends to make the mechanism appear complex, it was actually very simple and very reliable during use.

Pneumatics were extensively used, being employed for the retraction of the landing gear, the operation of the undercarriage doors, the wheel brakes, the centring of the nose wheel, and the flaps. It was also used to

Although ladders were needed to reach the Alvis Leonides engines they were readily accessible through the hinged panels (Percival Aircraft Ltd).

operate the air-intake shutters and the slow running cut-off valves fitted to the engine. The system was energized by two compressors, one on each engine. After passing through an anti-freezing unit, an oil and water trap and a filter, the air was stored at a pressure of 1,030 lb/sq in in bottles mounted in the nacelles. Each service was supplied through a valve which reduced the pressure to that required for the particular function for which it was to be used. An isolating valve, interconnected with the flying controls locking lever, cut off the supply to all services except that to the brakes.

In the air the Prince had a maximum speed of 222 mph and, with 58% power, cruised at 193 mph. The service ceiling was 24,800 ft, but with one engine out of action this was reduced to 10,000 ft. The wing area of 365 sq ft gave a wing loading of 29.2 lb/sq ft. The power loading was 10.24 lb/hp.

Extensive use was made of the 'rubber press' for the production of the ribs and frames but a new innovation was employed to form the curved panels used elsewhere. Previously, any panel requiring curvature in two or more planes had to be laboriously hand-beaten or rolled by highly-skilled panel-beaters. For the Prince the flat sheets were stretched over a former of the required shape by several high-pressure hydraulic rams. Such a method produced an item in minutes which otherwise would have taken skilled craftsmen hours of toil.

The unpainted prototype bearing the class B registration G-23-1 was first flown by Wg Cdr H. P. Powell (who had taken over the role of Chief Pilot after the resignation of Capt L. T. Carruthers) on 13 May 1948 and was successful from the start, the only modification necessary being the addition of a small dorsal fin. The ghastly deep and near-vertical windscreen was also replaced later by a more aesthetically pleasing and aerodynamically efficient shallower version.

On one occasion when landing after a test flight, the brakes failed and for some reason the propellers refused to go into reverse pitch. Faced with these problems Powell had no option but to overrun, finishing up in a cabbage patch tenderly nurtured by Hilda Rushden, the wife of the airport manager. The Prince suffered no damage but Hilda was most upset at having lost her supply of green vegetables.

The prototype received its full certificate of airworthiness and was registered to the company on 18 August 1948 as G-ALCM and given a livery of silver overall with blue lettering and flashes outlined in white. Further wind tunnel tests were conducted at Toulouse in September which proved of benefit, and a very confident management laid down a production line of ten aircraft.

The prototype continued its service with the company as a test and demonstration aeroplane until it was finally dismantled at Luton in July 1956 after eight years of useful work. The first production aircraft, registered to the company as G-ALFZ on 18 January 1949, in a livery of silver overall with green flashes and lettering, took off in March of the same year on the start of a 25,000 mile proving flight with Capt R. W. Hornall in command. During this flight to the Cape, tropical trials were undertaken at Khartoum, Nairobi

and Accra. This exploit was followed by a demonstration and proving flight by the second production aircraft, G-ALJA. During this tour to Bombay via the Near East, the Prince was flown continuously under simulated airline conditions and schedules. Both flights were highly successful and few, if any, replacement parts were needed.

The first production aircraft, G-ALFZ, was eventually sold to the Brazilian airline Aeronorte for whom it was converted to the Prince 2 standard with accommodation for ten passengers. Temporarily fitted with an auxiliary fuel tank of 100 gallon capacity in the cabin, the machine left Prestwick on 7 August 1950 bearing the temporary registration PP-XEG. The delivery flight was via Keflavik, Bluie West One, Goose Bay, Dorval, Miami and Jamaica. On its arrival in Brazil it was given the permanent registration PP-NBA under which it flew for two years before crashing on 9 March when it was damaged beyond economical repair.

The second production aircraft, G-ALJA, was purchased by the Shell Refining & Marketing Co Ltd and in July 1950 was transferred to Singapore where it flew under the registration VR-SDB. Some time later it was based in Borneo and while there carried the registration VR-UBD.

Soon after its introduction, the aircraft was upgraded to Prince 2 standard. The spars were strengthened and the all-up weight increased from 10,650 lb to 11,000 lb. Apart from this difference the aircraft was identical in all respects to its earlier sister. The ultimate example, designated the Prince 3, was exhibited at the 1952 SBAC show. The all-up weight remained at 11,000 lb but more powerful Alvis Leonides 502/4 of 550 hp were installed. With these the maximum speed increased to 229 mph and the cruising speed to 212 mph. With the undercarriage and flaps extended the stalling speed was 75 mph. These changes increased the wing loading to 30.1 lb/sq ft but the power loading, due to the more powerful engines,

The Sea Prince C.Mk 1 was identical to the civil aircraft and equipped to carry eight passengers and a crew of two. It was flown to America in July 1951 (Percival Aircraft Ltd).

decreased to 10 lb/hp.

The Prince was an immediate success. The Royal Navy purchased a number which were used as communications aircraft, the version being designated the Sea Prince C.Mk1 – not to be confused with the Sea Prince T.Mk1 which was a totally different aircraft. The first example of the Sea Prince C.Mk1 first flew on 24 March 1950 and one of the type was used by the Flag Officer (Air) Home as his aerial barge. It was finished in a livery of deep blue overall with the national markings outlined by a thin white line. The serial number, WF 137, was carried in white lettering. Bill Shakespear and his staff expended many hours burnishing the machine, their effort imparting a sheen which did justice to a Rolls-Royce!

Another Sea Prince C.Mk1 in standard silver livery and carrying the serial number WF 136 was used by the British Joint Services Mission in America. These service aeroplanes were identical to their civil counterparts but carried additional equipment and were fitted with the Goodrich pulsating de-icing shoes on the leading edges of all flying surfaces.

Shortly after the prototype had flown, the company was approached by Hunting Aerosurveys Ltd, another member of the Hunting Group, to see if it would be feasible to adapt the Prince to meet their specific needs. The result was the Survey Prince, the first of the type bearing the registration letters G-ALRY and a livery of silver overall with red decoration. It was exhibited at the SBAC show held at Farnborough in September 1949.

Although a basic airframe was used, the modifications necessary to convert it to the survey role were such that the issue of a new project number, P54, was warranted.

A new, deeper and longer nose portion was married to a much modified fuselage. The new nose section accommodated an observer-cum-photographer and a pilot, the second pilot's position being deleted. Through optically-flat panels incorporated in the glazing at the extreme front the observer had an unobstructed view approaching 130° from a point well above the horizon. To give access to this station half the instrument panel was removed. The pilot was stationed on the port side and to lighten his duties was provided with a Smiths SEP1 electronic auto-pilot.

The floor of the cabin was modified to incorporate two camera hatches with pneumatically-operated doors and the fourth window on both sides was replaced by a circular port for the oblique cameras. In spite of these modifications the cabin could be readily converted to accommodate eight or ten passengers. The duration was enhanced by increasing the capacity of the fuel tanks to 226 gallons.

On 2 February 1950 G-ALRY, flown by John Saffrey the senior pilot of Hunting Aerosurveys, left Bovingdon on a positioning flight of 3,200 miles to Sharjah on the Persian Gulf to initially undertake a four-month oil pros-pecting survey in Persia, but the tour was eventually extended to include surveys in Turkey, Siam and Kuwait. The Prince was seconded to Hunting Surveys' East African subsidiary at Nairobi in May 1956 and while based there operated with the temporary registration VP-KNN. The aircraft returned to Great Britain in January 1959 and three months later, in March, was sold to the French company Sté Protection Aéroportée who operated the machine extensively from Le Bourget on radar calibration duties. It then carried the registration F-BJAJ.

Three further Survey Princes were constructed, two being ordered by the Tanganyikan Government. They were registered to them as VR-TBC and VR-TBD, the former carrying the name 'Prince Charles'. The third example, HB-HOF, was delivered to Eidgenössischen Vermessungsdirektion, a Swiss survey company.

The Prince was widely used by the Shell Refining & Marketing Co Ltd, the Aviation Department being managed by the late Sir Douglas Bader who, later, was appointed managing director when Shell Aviation was formed in 1958. He was a popular and frequent visitor to Luton and personally collected all, or most, of the eight Princes operated by his company. When he collected the first machine he enquired of Jack Lavender as to whether the compass had been swung. When assured that it had he remarked: '. . . You'd better swing it again with me in the cockpit . . . I think you'll find my tin legs will make quite a difference.'

A brief history of their first aeroplane, G-ALJA, has been outlined earlier in this chapter. Their next two Princes, both registered to them on 23 March 1950 as G-ALWG and G-ALWH were destined to serve in Venezuela, the former as YV-P-AEO and carrying the name 'El Vijeo'; the latter as YV-P-AEQ. G-ALWG was fitted-out as a six-seat executive aircraft and the latter as an eight-seat passenger-cum-freighter. Both machines arrived in Maracaibo, Venezuela on 18 April 1950, covering the 6,500 mile flight from Luton in fourteen days, the route being the same as that taken earlier by PP-XEG.

In February 1953 G-ALWH returned to England and assumed its original registration. It was then sold to the Sperry Gyroscope Co and operated by them until January 1961 when it was acquired by the Decca Navigation Company and based at Biggin Hill. Shell's fourth aeroplane, G-AMKK, was registered on 28 March 1952 and in June of the same year was transferred to Singapore where it flew as VR-SDR before going to Borneo as VR-UDR, the same service as performed by their first Prince.

Their next aeroplane, G-AMLW, served from 26 May 1952 until March 1959, first in Venezuela where it flew as YV-P-AEB from August, until it was stationed in Australia in August 1957 with the registration VH-AGF. It was then sold to Société Protection Aéroportée of France and given the registration F-BJAI.

The final three aeroplanes ordered by the Shell Refining & Marketing Co Ltd were delivered in October and November 1952, the first of the batch, G-AMLX on the 8th, G-AMLY on the 22nd, and the last, G-AMLZ, on 14 November. After being extensively used in Europe G-ALMX was flown to Borneo in the March of 1955 where it was re-registered VR-UDA. Venezuela was the first base for G-AMLY where it was given the registration YV-P-AEC on its arrival in December. It returned to Great Britain and its original registration in 1955 after a very short tour of overseas duties and was sold to Martin-Baker Aircraft Ltd of Denham who used the machine to ferry their executive staff in connection with their many contracts. It was then upgraded to Prince 4 standard and passed through Bahrein on 3 September on its way to serve with the British Malayan Petroleum Company Limited in Borneo, where it was registered VR-UDC.

Records indicate that G-AMLZ remained in England and was operated by Shell for just under two years, until August 1954, after which the ownership changed to W. F. Martin who based the machine at Tollerton. He retained the Prince before selling it to Stewart, Smith & Co, who flew it from Blackbushe from June 1956 until October 1968. After this twelve-year stint G-AMLZ passed to the ownership of T. M. Clutterbuck and was based at Leavesden.

During the period when Bader was collecting the Princes ordered by the Shell Company, the publications department was temporarily housed in the old RAFVR watch hut situated in the middle of the apron, a position which afforded a commanding view of all activities, idyllic in the warm summer months but not so during the winter when snow would blow in through gaps in the floor boards, the linoleum covering having long since disappeared. On this particular day, Bader had just completed an acceptance flight and parked the Prince almost in front of our office. He then walked over to the office of Jack Lavender in the flight shed to complete the paperwork. Soon after he had departed, a steam roller which was being used by contractors to compact rubble on an apron extension chuffed over to take on water.

The driver, intent on reaching this essential supply before his boiler ran dry, took a short cut and passed under the wing quite forgetting that he was preceeded by a rather tall smokestack. This struck the leading edge and drove it backward almost to the front spar!

I knew that Bader was very adept in the use of his tin legs, and that he had an excellent command of basic Anglo-Saxon; both were amply demonstrated! He covered the fifty yards from the hangar to his damaged aeroplane – for which he had just signed and therefore was responsible – at a speed which would have done credit to an Olympic runner. And the dressing down he gave to the unfortunate driver was beyond description. Although this may have relieved the tension that had obviously built up inside Sir Douglas on seeing the damage the substantial smokestack had inflicted on his aeroplane, it had little effect on the driver . . . he was stone deaf!

Three specially modified and equipped Prince 3 aircraft, G-AMKW, G-AMKX and G-AMKY were supplied to the Ministry of Civil Aviation. They were extensively equipped for the calibration of airfield radio, radar and navigational aids and had longer and deeper nose sections with a radar scanner in the extreme nose behind a glass-fibre nose-cap. The aeroplanes were registered on 16 July, 3 November and 12 December 1952 as G-AMKW, G-AMKX and G-AMKY respectively. After a service life of some eighteen

years, all were withdrawn from active use in late 1969 and 70, finishing their days passively with the Stanstead Fire Section.

One of the early production aircraft, G-AKYE, was first registered to the company on 30 April 1951 but sold in the following month to the Brazilian airline Aeronorte (who were already operating PP-NBA the ex G-ALFZ). It was flown by them carrying the registration PP-NFB until the July of 1954. It then passed to the ownership of R. B. Archer of Rio de Janiero and the registration PT-ASW.

Three specially modified Prince 3 aircraft were supplied to the Ministry of Civil Aviation for the calibration of airfield radar, radio and navigational aids. G-AMKY, the last of the trio and was delivered in December 1952 (Flight).

Special hatches were installed in the underside of the fuselage of G-ALRY for the vertical cameras (Percival Aircraft Ltd).

The SBAC show of 1952 was used to exhibit the first Prince 3. This was fitted with Alvis Leonides 502/4 engines which had been developed to give 550 hp. With these the performance improved, raising the economical cruising speed to 197 mph and the maximum speed to 229 mph. The all-up weight was also increased to 11,500 lb which raised the wing loading to 31.5 lb/sq ft and the power loading to 10.45 lb/hp. The machine was fitted out as a six-seat executive transport for the South African Iron & Steel Industrial Organisation and based at Wonderboom where it flew as ZS-DGX.

Two further Survey Princes were built and registered as G-AMNT and G-AMOT. The former, G-AMNT, was based on the Prince 3 specification but, being a survey version, was designated the Prince 3A of which only one example was built. It was given Thai Air Force livery and the serial number Q1-1/98 and ferried to Thailand under British markings in March 1952. It undertook survey work for the Mapping Organisation of the Ministry of Defence.

The second Survey Prince was ordered by Hunting Aerosurveys Ltd to fulfill a contract in Canada and was equipped with an airborne magnetometer. The aircraft was powered by two Alvis Leonides 502/5 engines, each giving 560 hp; the designation Prince 3D recognising this modification. A year later, after completing its tour of duty in Canada, G-AMOT (as it had been registered) returned to the United Kingdom where minor modifications were incorporated. These included the fitting of a more efficient braking system. The machine was then flown out to Kenya where it undertook a survey to locate deposits of uranium but on 6 June 1958, six years after being registered, it was destroyed in a forced landing in the jungle near the Mackinnion Road Airfield in Kenya.

One of the last Prince aircraft built was delivered to the Standard Motor Company being registered to them on 30 September 1952 as G-AMPR. It was based at Baginton where it was used as an executive transport sumptuously furnished with six luxurious seats, a well-appointed cloakroom and bar with the walls covered by a Regency-stripe cloth of pale blue and white; the design being the creation of a well-known interior decorator.

Four years later the aeroplane was given a thorough overhaul and, in February 1956, was sold to the Tanganyika Government carrying the name 'Prince Hal' and the registration VR-TBN. After serving for six years it was

This interior view of 'LRY shows the Williamson OSC camera installation which was heated to prevent freezing (Percival Aircraft Ltd).

The second Survey Prince supplied to Hunting Aerosurveys was registered as G-AMOT and fitted with an airborne Magnetometer. The machine was destroyed in a forced landing in Kenya (Hunting Aircraft Ltd).

The re-designed nose of the P54 Survey Prince gave the observer-cum-photographer an unobstructed view approaching 130° from a point well above the horizon (Hunting Aerosurveys Ltd).

sold to Polynesian Airlines and given the registration ZK-TYN and, in company with VR-TBD – the ex-Tanganyikan Government Survey Prince that had been re-registered as ZK-BYD – was ferried from Dar-es-Salaam to Samoa in February 1962.

The Prince was basically an efficient civil aeroplane designed to meet the requirements of civil operators throughout the world although a number were sold to Governments overseas including that of Australia who purchased two of the type. It also had much potential which lead to the aeroplane being developed for miliary use. This eventually ousted the civil product and the last Prince left the production lines in 1953 after twenty-six of the type had been built.

Before closing this chapter on the Prince it would be worthwhile to recount an incident that befell Dick Wheldon, the Chief Pilot appointed after the resignation of Wg Cdr Powell. While preparing to land after a routine test flight the audio-warning sounded, warning the pilot that the undercarriage was not locked down. At the same time it was noticed that the undercarriage indicator lamps had failed. Although it was possible to check the position of the main undercarriage, the same was not possible for the nose wheel – that was invisible! Dick therefore instructed his observer to contact the Control Tower by radio to request visual confirmation on the state of his wayward landing gear. Unfortunately that had also failed! After a brief discussion the problem was solved. During a low pass, a boot – supplied by one of the crew – containing a hastily scribbled note, was hurled from the aeroplane. Visual inspection was made from the ground and a 'green' was given. The landing was uneventful.

CHAPTER 9

THE SEA PRINCE, PEMBROKE AND PRESIDENT

From experience gained from the Sea Prince C.Mk I the Royal Navy was quick to realise the potential of the aircraft and issued a specification for its conversion to a flying classroom in which aircrews could be trained in the use of radio, radar and navigation and in particular the techniques used in anti-submarine warfare. A series of layout drawings were prepared showing the disposition of the proposed equipment and the redesign of the airframe began under the design code P57.

Structurally the Sea Prince T.Mk I as it was officially designated, was identical to its civil counterpart but with certain, relatively minor, modifications to adapt it to a military role. A longer nose section, similar to that fitted to the Prince 3 but modified to house the radar and sonabouy equipment, was married to a modified rear fuselage which accommodated three pupils and an instructor (all facing aft), their desks, radar, radio and sonabouy equipment with the necessary hatches for deployment.

Additional aerials were installed and the escape hatches were modified to incorporate built-in containers in which inflatable life-rafts were stowed.

The single wheel of the main undercarriage was replaced by twin wheels and the unit was redesigned to withstand a descent velocity approaching 12 ft/sec. The engine nacelles were increased in length to smooth the air flow over the empennage units and to accommodate the modified under-carriage. These changes increased the all-up weight to 11,500 lb which was later enhanced by 350 lb to give a final all-up weight of 11,850 lb and with a fuel capacity of 106 gallons the Sea Prince T.Mk I had a still air range of 500 nautical miles when flown at a constant speed of 150 knots.

The first of the breed flew on 28 June 1951 and was the harbinger of 42 aeroplanes eventually delivered to the Royal Navy to replace its ageing Avro Ansons, remaining in service for over a quarter of a century. In addition to the T.Mk I, four Sea Prince C.Mk II aircraft were delivered. Although outwardly identical, the internal arrangement, being a communications version, was completely different having a well-upholstered cabin equipped with eight rearward facing seats plus a crew of two. Apart from the length which increased to 46 ft, the overall dimensions were identical to the Prince.

The Royal Air Force had also earmarked the Prince as an aircraft with much potential, their multi-role version, when it entered service, being known as the Pembroke C.Mk I. Under the design code P66 the airframe was re-stressed to take an all-up weight of 13,500 lb. This entailed increasing the span of the wing by 8 ft 6 in to give a total span of 64 ft 6 in, the increase being achieved by adding extension panels at the tips which inset the ailerons and increased the wing area to 400 sq ft. This included the slotted flaps which, as on the other versions, amounted to 38.6 sq ft. The wing loading, in spite of the larger wing, increased to 33.75 lb/sq ft.

When taking off fully loaded from a hard runway at sea level, the Pembroke could reach a height of 50 ft in 790 yards with an initial rate of climb of 1,500 ft/min and if one engine failed during take off it was capable of climbing to an altitude of 1,000 ft at a rate of 50 ft/min provided that the propeller of the inoperative engine was feathered. It was not necessary to retract the undercarriage to achieve this, but if it was raised, the rate of climb improved to 210 ft/min. In both emergencies the flaps were left in the take off position. Under normal conditions an altitude of 6,000 ft could be attained in 5.6 minutes and to reach 20,000 ft – 2,000 ft short of its service ceiling – took 34.4 minutes.

Although a larger and heavier aeroplane than the ultimate Prince 3 by some 2,500 lb all-up, the maximum speed of 220 mph was only 3 mph slower than its civil counterpart but, when cruising with the maximum rich mixture setting, was some 12 mph faster at 209 mph. The most economical cruising speed was 150 mph which returned a still air range of 1,030 miles.

Apart from being stressed for a higher all-up weight and the extension panels at the wing tips, the general construction followed the pattern set in the previous versions. All control systems (flying, engine and pneumatics) were located under the floor of the crew compartment and transferred to the ceiling over the cabin area, the change of direction by means of pullies and bell-crank levers being at the bulkhead between the two compartments. The cables and pneumatic pipes were protected by consoles (on both sides) in which the radio equipment was also mounted.

The interior was heated by air collected by scoops mounted on the engine nacelles. The air then passed through intensifier tubes situated in the exhaust system and thence, through lagged ducts, to grills in the walls of the cabin at floor level and in the crew's compartment where it was discharged; the temperature of the air entering the interior being regulated by valves located in the leading edge of the wings and controlled by handwheels in the cockpit. Two heating systems were fitted, one on each engine, and were entirely independent so that, in the event of an engine failure, an adequate supply of hot air was still available.

The cabin was ventilated by an air intake on top of the fuselage which supplied air to two ducts forming the inboard rail of the two luggage racks. Individually controlled punkah louvres were fitted at each seat position and stale air was extracted through controllable grills in the ceiling of the cabin with an independent extraction duct in the toilet compartment. An H-type inflatable five-man dinghy was stowed in a container in each of the two escape hatches built into the top of the fuselage.

When operating in the communications role for the Royal Air Force, eight fully adjustable rearward-facing seats, designed to withstand a force of 15 G, were fitted and stowage for luggage was provided in compartments at the rear of the cabin and in the nose. The seats could be quickly and easily removed when it was necessary to operate the aircraft in a different role.

Because the Pembroke was used by the air forces of a number of nations, the roles in which it was required to operate were many and varied. Up to twelve passengers in forward or rearward-facing seats could be accommodated in the 620 cu ft cabin with a floor strong enough to take the concentrated load of a spare Leonides engine on a pallet. And the door was big enough to allow it to enter freely! Strong lashing points were built into the structure with a strong point opposite the cabin door for the safety harness of the crew when supply dropping. A separate strong point was used for the static lines.

All versions were capable of being quickly and easily converted to aerial ambulances capable of transporting up to nine stretcher cases and an attendant. Webbing straps to support the inboard handles of the stretchers were stowed in housings built into the ceiling of the cabin. When in use these clipped into the seat anchorage fittings in the floor. Retractable fittings, flush with the upholstery when not in use, were built into the walls to support and secure the outboard handles.

Following an intensive sales campaign (with some assistance from NATO) the Pembroke was sold to Rhodesia, Denmark, West Germany, Sweden, Finland and Belgium; the aircraft for the two last-named countries had transparent nose-caps with optically-flat panels. To give access to this crew position, the flying controls for the second pilot and part of the instrument panel was removed, a facility built into all versions.

The ability of the structure to absorb punishment was amply demonstrated when Joe Arnold, one of the test pilots, was forced to abort his landing, almost at the point of touch-down, when the pilot of a machine from the flying club taxied across his path. Joe immediately opened his throttles, retracted the undercarriage and made another circuit. From then on things went awry! For some unknown reason the undercarriage warning horn failed to operate and the staff of the control tower did not observe that the approaching aeroplane still had its wheels up! The Pembroke slithered for several hundred yards before coming to a halt with its wings perfectly level and the undamaged propellers still ticking over! Damage was limited to the bottom of the frames and the skin over the cabin area. This took but a few days to repair and the aircraft was soon flying again.

The ultimate version of the series was the President, a civil version and structurally identical with the Pembroke. To quote from a brochure issued by the Company in August 1956, '. . . it will be clear to the discerning operator that the experience which has been gained in the construction of its successful predecessors has enabled Hunting Percival Aircraft Limited to produce in the President an aeroplane which combines to the best advantage the economically desirable features of ease of operation and maintenance, coupled with rugged construction, outstanding performance and extreme versatility'. In spite of the high ideals it was not a success and only six of the type were built – and one of those was a Pembroke conversion undertaken by another company!

The first President, initially designated the Prince V, flew on 26 August

All the Prince 3 aircraft supplied to the Ministry of Civil Aviation had glass-fibre nose caps behind which was mounted the radar scanner.

1956 carrying the registration G-AOJG and was exhibited at the SBAC show in a livery of pale cream and maroon. When Bill Shakespear was applying the cheat-lines over the nose he had some difficulty in the alignment so, having designed the paint scheme, my assistance was called for. With the help of another colleague one side was masked-up, the other being roughly aligned before taking our lunch break. When we returned we found, to our horror, that Bill and his staff – who had taken an earlier break – had assumed that the job was compete and had sprayed it!

After being fitted out as an executive aircraft with six seats, G-AOJG left Luton on 29 April 1956 to undertake a European sales tour after which it continued to be used as a demonstration and general purpose aircraft until it was sold to the Danish Air Force. It was delivered to them via Southend on 4 July 1959 carrying the serial number 697 – later changed to OY-AVA.

Resulting from the sales tour, three Presidents were ordered by the Spanish air line TAE, of Bilbao. They had intended to use the aeroplanes on internal services in Spain and the Balearic Islands but after the first aircraft had been completed and finished in the livery of the company, the order was cancelled. For almost two years the three machines remained at Luton but eventually the first, as EC-APA, was sold to the Sudanese Air Force. Bearing the serial number '10' it was ferried through Southend on 28 January 1959.

For a time the third aircraft – EC-APC – was re-registered as G-AVPJ and used by the Company but, together with its sister, was also sold to the

Sudanese Air Force; both being ferried through Southend on 3 March 1960 with EC-APB bearing the serial number '11' and 'APC the number '12'. Soon after the arrival of the two Presidents, number '10' (ex 'APA) was flown back to Luton where it was refurbished and registered to Hunting Aircraft Ltd as G-ARCN on 1 September 1960. It remained at the Company until March 1962 when it was sold to the Bristol Aeroplane Co (later part of the British Aircraft Corporation) and based at Filton where it was used as a communications aircraft making frequent flights to the Continent during the period of Concorde co-operation before being withdrawn from use in October 1970.

The Ministry of Civil Aviation, who already had three Princes in their fleet, took delivery of a President in 1958. It was registered as G-AMPO on 29 September and, based with the Flying Unit at Stanstead, flew for twelve years before being withdrawn from use in July 1970. Three years later it was presented to No. 1163 Squadron of the Air Training Corps at Earls Colne.

The President that wasn't, started life as a Pembroke. It was the thirteenth of the type to be built and after serving with the Empire Test Pilot's School at Farnbrough was put on the disposal list. It was acquired by the Air Navigation and Trading Company of Squires Gate who converted it to President standard. It entered the civil register as G-APNL on 29 June 1958 but whether it was ever used in its civil role is unknown as the records merely state 'scrapped'.

Although replaced by the Jetstream, the Pembroke continued to serve in the Royal Air Force for more than 30 years after first being introduced. About a dozen redundant Pembrokes were exported to the United States of America where they found a ready market with the drug-running fraternity.

Although the Prince was offered with floats, as depicted in this model displayed at the 1952 SBAC show, none was built.

The Sea Prince T.Mk 1 differed from the civil Prince by having extended engine nacelles, twin wheels to the main undercarriage and a revised nose (Flight).

Many were destroyed in crashes resulting from the 'hairy' low-level flying necessary to avoid radar interception or were impounded by Federal Agents and by 1981 only three remained in an airworthy condition.

A more legitimate pursuit was reported in 1981. Two Pembrokes were being operated by Aircrane West of Santa Cruz on behalf of the University of California who were undertaking a survey of the bird and mammal population off the west coast of America. A third Pembroke was used to provide spares. Two of the aircraft, coded RM2 and RM12 once belonged to the Belgian Air Force; the third began its service life in July 1956 as XF796.

It was one of six special photographic reconnaissance Pembroke C(PR)I aircraft built for the Royal Air Force and first served with No. 81 Squadron in Malaya. in 1962 it flew with the Far East Communication Squadron and then with No. 60 Squadron. To extend the fatigue life of the airframe the wings were resparred (as were most of the Pembrokes serving in the RAF) in July 1970 and it continued to serve for a further six years before being placed on the disposal list by No. 23 Maintenance Squadron. It was purchased by A. F. Nicholson and registered as G-BFKK but rising fuel costs forced its disposal.

It was purchased by Aircrane West where it flew in company with RM2, both sporting their original livery, on environmental flights on behalf of the University at heights barely exceeding 100 ft altitude.

Comprehensive operating and maintenance manuals were required for all aircraft built under Government contracts. These included chapters detailing the removal and installation procedures for various components and units. This entailed discussion with the design staff and, if necessary, a demonstration of the proposed method in the workshops during which notes were taken and sketches made.

Among my tasks was the installation of the flexible fuel tanks within the special compartments built into the wing. The flexible tanks were held in

Belgian Pembrokes under construction at Luton (Percival Aircraft Ltd).

A Pembroke of the Royal Swedish Air Force awaits delivery in front of the 'new' control tower at Luton (Hunting Percival Aircraft Ltd).

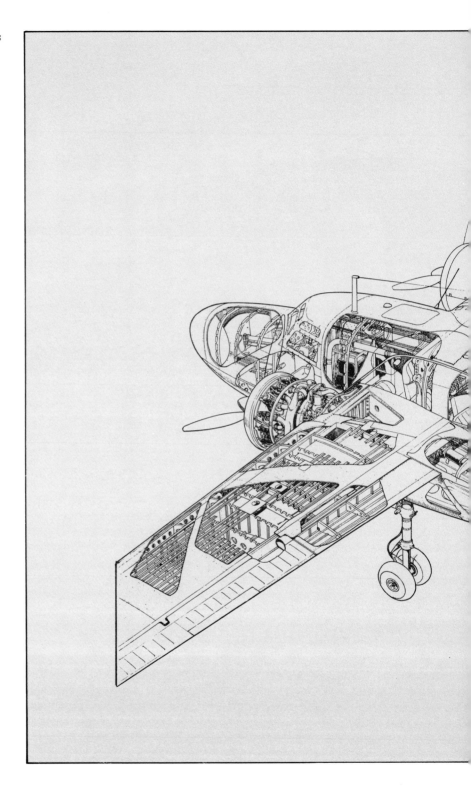

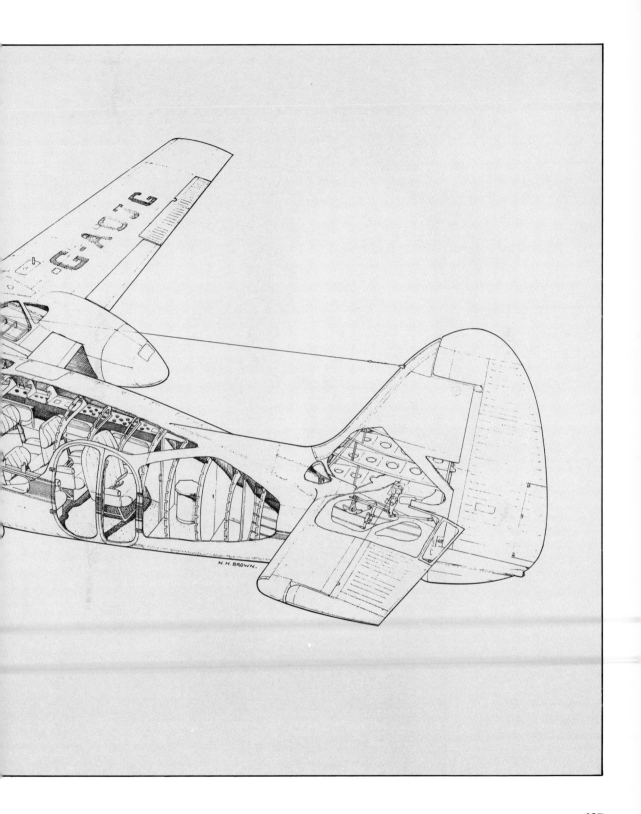

W. H. BROWN.

127

Pembrokes of the Royal Swedish Air Force had accommodation for ten passengers in rearward facing seats (Hunting Percival Aircraft Ltd).

The Pembroke could be quickly converted to an aerial ambulance for six casualties and an attendant (Percival Aircraft Ltd).

position by nylon cords which passed alternately between spigots on the tank skin and others located on the upper skin of the compartment; the lacing being to a set pattern to ensure proper rigidity. When completed the nylon cords were pulled tight, wound around toggles attached to their ends and finally clipped into a tray mounting the filler neck and the contents sender unit. This tray was the last item to be installed and the aperture into which it fitted was used to insert the bag-tank initially.

I had spent several hours with the designer and to satisfy myself that I fully understood the procedure outlined, decided to undertake the installation myself. Arrangements were made for this to be done, but after normal working hours to ensure that production was not interrupted.

The last Sea Princes in service in the Royal Navy were with 750 Squadron Culdrose.

A Pembroke of the Luftwaffe with the well-known Bedfordshire landmark in the background (Hunting Percival Aircraft Ltd).

129

A Pembroke of the Royal Belgian Air Force, one of the many members of NATO to use the aircraft (Flight).

The first President, G-AOJG, after being flown as a demonstrator and general purpose aircraft for three years by the company, was sold to the Danish Air Force in 1959. Later it was given the civil registration OY-AVA (Flight).

Thus, in a dark and deserted assembly shop I made my way to the aeroplane allocated and climbed on to the top of the wing to begin my task. I pushed the flexible tank into the wing and spread it neatly over the bottom of the compartment. Next my groping fingers sought and found the end of the cords which was then passed through the spigots, first on the compartment roof and then on the tank. 'Easy!' I thought, 'A piece of cake!' I continued lacing, changing my position for comfort as the nylon cord gradually worked toward the tank aperture. At last all the spigots were laced and I was ready for the final operation, that of pulling the cords tight and inserting the filler tray.

But when I tried to withdraw my arms I found they were trapped at the elbows! I was firmly held in a crouching posture some twelve feet above the ground with no-one in sight to render assistance! I tried to ease my body

The President, EC-APA flanked by a Luftwaffe Pembroke and the first President, was built for the Spanish airline TAE. It was not delivered to them and eventually was sold to the Sudanese (Hunting Percival Aircraft Ltd).

The President was a logical development of the Pembroke which entered service with the RAF in 1952 (Hunting Percival Aircraft Ltd).

around to release my arms but my fingers became ensnared in the lines. Fighting the panic which was rapidly approaching I methodically unlaced the cord until, some thirty minutes later, I was thankfully able to withdraw my aching limbs.

The following morning I met the designer and explained the difficulty. 'Sorry cock!' he said with a slow grin, 'I thought that might happen . . . try it this way!'

CHAPTER 10

THE PROVOST

The Prentice had completely revolutionised the principles of *ab initio* flying training and had set the seal of approval on the basic ideas formulated at the Empire Central Flying School. With the increasing complexity of Service aircraft it was, and still is, vital that only the best of student pilots should receive the expensive and time-consuming training necessary for them to fly the complicated and expensive operational aeroplanes.

The simple 'any-one can fly' basic training aircraft formerly used allowed virtually all and sundry to enter the flying training channel and it was accepted that many would fall by the wayside during the later stages. This was not only wasteful on resources but, having flown solo at the elementary stage, a student pilot, having failed to achieve the standards required later in the course, invariably felt a great sense of injustice. The new formula with its more complex aircraft, enabled unsuitable students to be suspended from the course at an early stage. This eliminated a possible loss of morale and considerably reduced unnecessary expenditure of the instructor's time and aircraft hours.

During the time the Prentice was in service use, the flying training schools of the Royal Air Force had ample opportunity to observe its operation under the new system and formulate their own ideas of what changes or improvements were required. From these observations the specification T.16/48 was prepared. In this the authorities outlined the fundamental requirements but left the designer far more flexibility than had

The prototype Provost T.Mk 1, powered by an Armstrong Siddeley Cheetah engine, in its original form with the long tailwheel strut (Percival Aircraft Ltd)

Another prototype Provost T.Mk 1 after the rear fuselage had been lowered by inseting a gusset immediately behind the cockpit. The tailwheel has also been replaced by a shorter strut version (Percival Aircraft Ltd).

previously been given; the aircraft industry was, in effect, left to use its ingenuity to produce a suitable solution.

Over thirty submissions were made by the industry to the tender but, as the directors of Percival Aircraft had such faith in the design produced by Arthur Bage meeting the new concept of service pilot training, by the time the specification was issued, the Provost – as it was eventually named – had reached an advanced stage in its construction as a private venture. Arthur Bage's conception so nearly accorded to the specification that little change was required to meet it in full. Apart from the Provost, one other design, the HPR.2 submitted by Handley-Page (Reading) Ltd (formerly Miles Aircraft Ltd) was selected for evaluation.

The initial design proposals envisaged the installation of a de Havilland Gipsy Queen engine but, through the experience with the Merganser, this was changed to the Armstrong Siddeley Cheetah 17 air-cooled radial engine. This was fortuitous as the T.16/48 specification stipulated that type of engine.

Allocated the design number P56, the prototype, carrying the serial number WE522, first flew in the hands of Dick Wheldon on 23 February 1950. From the start it displayed the attributes of a winner. Although the early flight trials had proved the general handling qualities to be good there was an indication that some improvement could be gained in elevator response. This was achieved by lowering the rear fuselage about its bottom line by inserting a 'gusset' immediately aft of the cockpit and shortening the length of the tailwheel fork. With this modification the aircraft was stable in all flight conditions of normal flight.

The controls were pleasantly harmonised and the very effective ailerons gave a rate of roll of over 90° per second. Although it was comparatively easy to fly and land, the light controls gave handling qualities reminiscent of the best type of fighter then in service with the Royal Air Force.

The prototype was demonstrated at the SBAC shown held at Farnborough in 1950 where its performance was more than comparable with its competitor, the Handley-Page HPR.2 which, by that time, had been fitted with the more powerful Leonides engine.

With an all-up weight of 4,050 lb the Provost had a wing loading of 18 lb/sq ft and a power loading of 9.64 lb/hp. It had a maximum speed of 177 mph, and cruised at 153 mph. The stalling speed with the flaps down was 64 mph. A service ceiling of 17,500 ft could be easily attained and with an initial rate of climb of 1,360 ft/min, an altitude of 10,000 feet could be reached in a little over ten minutes.

Two further Provosts were built for evaluation and one was fitted with the supercharged Alvis Leonides 25 air-cooled radial engine of 550 hp driving a three-bladed propeller through a reduction gear. With this fitted the all-up weight increased to 4,250 lb which raised the wing loading to

Variations on a theme. The Cheetah powered WE530 formates on the Leonides powered prototype carrying the class 'B' registration G-23-1. The latter was selected to replace the Prentice (Percival Aircraft Ltd).

Cut-away drawing of the Provost from the original literature issued on this aircraft by the company.

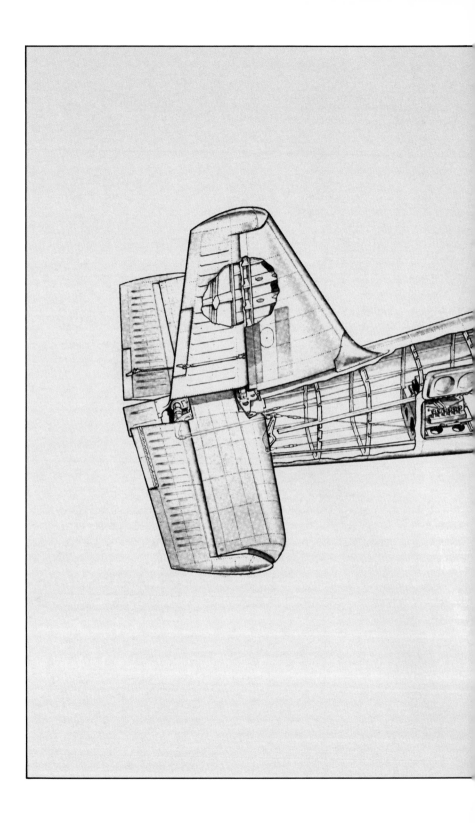

J. CRAWLEY

The side-by-side seating made the Provost an ideal vehicle for armament training. This is the armed version and was fitted with two .303 machine guns and a camera gun. A variety of under-wing stores could be carried as alternatives to the six 60 lb rocket projectiles shown (Percival Aircraft Ltd).

19.85 lb/sq ft, but the more powerful engine reduced the power loading to 7.73 lb/hp. The maximum speed was increased by 23 mph giving a top speed of 200 mph and the cruising speed raised to 170 mph, an improvement of 17 mph. There was also a nominal increase in the stalling speed of 3 mph. Apart from the improved speeds, the initial rate of climb to the enhanced service ceiling of 22,500 ft and an altitude of 10,000 ft could be attained in seven minutes. This extended, in effect, the duration of the instructional period by enabling a safe height for aerobatics to be reached quickly.

The third prototype flying under the class B registration G-23-1 was used extensively to prove the Leonides installation. During the early test flights with this engine it was found that with the conventional cowlings there was uneven cooling of the cylinders. The chord of the cowlings was increased and although some improvement was gained, it was not perfect. After further experimentation two ducts, colloquially dubbed the 'elephant's ears', were fitted to both sides of the fuselage through which the cooling air was discharged.

Although this solved one problem it presented another! Almost from day-to-day the handling characteristics varied, usually after the cowlings had been removed for servicing. This caused much 'head-scratching' amongst the design staff but a methodical analysis of the facts eventually established the fault to lie in the profile of the ducts. When the cowlings were removed the profile of the ducts had been slightly distorted and this, coupled with the velocity and volume of the air being discharged, was sufficient to create an asymetric air-flow over the empennage. The addition of suitable supports soon rectified the fault. Following the extensive trials with G-23-1 all three prototype aircraft were fitted with the Alvis Leonides.

The Provost T.Mk I was a low-wing monoplane of robust, simple all-

metal construction designed for day and night flying training. A high standard of interchangeability between similar components enabled repairs to be made rapidly by the replacement of damaged or unserviceable units.

The fuselage was a semi-monocoque structure comprising frames, four 'U' section longerons and 'Z' section stringers all of which, with the exception of those interrupted by the access doors, were continuous; the frames being recessed to permit this. Within the rear fuselage a subsidiary floor was built on which were mounted the batteries, the Tunable Beam Approach (TBA) installation and the ten-channel radio; access to this equipment being through two hinged doors in the fuselage wall, one on the port side and the other to starboard. Two further panels in the bottom of the fuselage gave easy access to the equipment and installations beneath the cockpit floor.

A frame and a bulkhead (the latter having a large triangular door) at the rear of the cockpit area formed a 'V' (in the longitudinal plane) into which was built the rear attachment fittings for the wings; the main attachment points being mounted on a strong beam built into the bottom of the frame

Although the Provost was out of production, redundant RAF aircraft were purchased and refurbished for overseas customers, in this case Sudan (Flight).

coinciding with the rear of the windscreen.

The cockpit, accommodating a crew of two in side-by-side seating behind which was installed a strong tubular crash pylon, was totally enclosed by a transparent sliding and jettisonable hood incorporating amber screens for simulated cloud or night flying, first used on the Prentice. The system was found to be of particular value in countries where climatic conditions for cloud flying seldom occurred and in latitudes which, in summer, provided insufficient hours of darkness to meet the instrument flying programme.

The mainplanes, built in two sections, comprised a main and auxiliary spar, the latter mounting the attachments for the slotted flaps and ailerons; it also dissipated the loads imposed. Ribs pressed from light alloy progressed from a modified NACA 23015 section at the root to a NACA 4412 at the tip. They were attached to both spars and were recessed to allow the stringers of 'top-hat' section to extend continuously from the root outwards; the complete structure being covered by a skin of light alloy. In the leading edge of each wing, inboard of the undercarriage, was installed a flexible fire and crash-proof fuel tank of 33 gallons.

Both tanks were connected to a common light alloy collector tank mounted beneath the floor of the cockpit. In the tank was installed an electric immersion pump which supplemented the engine-driven pump and pressurised the injector unit during start-up.

The pneumatically-operated slotted flaps and the ailerons were similar in construction, each having 'D' section spars and ribs pressed from light alloy sheet and covered by a skin of Alcad, fluted to provide added rigidity. Both ailerons were fitted with trim tabs, that on the starboard side being adjustable in flight, the other on the ground only. The wings had a gross area of 214 sq/ft of which 18.94 sq/ft comprised the total flap area. Detachable wing tips housed the navigation lamps, the fairings moulded from clear plastic.

The tailplane, built as a single unit, was constructed around two light alloy spars which ran from tip-to-tip as did the 'Z' section stringers. The inter-spar and nose ribs were, as those of the wing, recessed to allow the stringers an unbroken run from tip-to-tip and the complete unit was covered by a stressed skin of Alclad sheet. The horn-balanced elevators were constructed as two separate and fully interchangeable units comprising a single 'D' section spar, pressed light alloy ribs with a small subsidiary spar extending over the span of each trim tab. The complete unit was covered by a fluted skin of light alloy. The elevators were interconnected by a torque tube of large diameter supported by ball-races mounted in forgings bolted to the rear spar of the tailplane.

The fin, covered by a stressed skin of light alloy, had twin spars, the one at the rear being at right-angles to the ribs and that at the front being inclined. When the Provost was first flown, the rear spar of the fin (and therefore the rudder hinge) was vertical. However, when the rear fuselage was lowered, the attachment points of the fin remained unaltered which effectively inclined the rudder hinge some 5° to the rear.

To the fin spars were riveted ribs pressed from light alloy with flanged lightening holes (as were all the ribs in the flying surfaces); the uppermost rib incorporating the attachment bracket for the pintle-hinge of the rudder. The rudder was also horn-balanced and built on a single spar of channel-section light alloy. To this was riveted light alloy ribs and, as on the elevators, a small subsidiary spar extended over the height of the servo tab with which the rudder was fitted. Pressed nose riblets supported the skin forward of the spar and the whole structure was covered by a skin of Alclad which, as on all the control surfaces, was fluted to provide added rigidity. The rudder hinged about two points, a pintle pin at the top, the bottom hinge being provided by the control lever mounted on ball-bearings in forgings bolted to the fuselage.

The undercarriage consisted of two long-stroke oleopneumatic mainwheel units and a tailwheel unit which incorporated a liquid-spring strut. The mainwheel units were mounted in forged brackets built into the wing structure forward of the main spar and held in position by a single flanged nut which made replacement a simple and easy matter in the event of accidental damage. Both legs were enclosed by quickly-detachable fairings with a small fixed fairing at the top in which was mounted the taxying lamps. Pneumatically-operated brakes were fitted and operated by control levers attached to the control columns; differential operation being applied by the rudder bars. Wheel alignment was held by forged knuckle-joints. The generous 11 ft 1½ in track gave remarkable stability during the landing and taxying.

The Alvis Leonides engine was attached to the airframe at four points and was mounted on triangulated tubular steel members incorporating a detachable front mounting ring which enabled the engine to be changed as a unit or as a complete power unit. The cowlings were quickly and easily removable; the side panels being secured by 'hook-and-toggle' type fasteners. The top and bottom sub-panels were also quickly detachable, that at the bottom incorporating the oil cooler and air-intake assembly which was fitted with a large dry filter element. The oil cooler was capable of controlling the temperature of the oil under arctic or tropical conditions, the flow of air being regulated by a manually-operated flap incorporated within the outlet duct.

The entire oil system, including the 6 gallon tank with a built-in 'hot-well' to enable the engine to be quickly warmed up, was installed forward of the firewall. A negative-G valve assembly was also fitted within the tank to ensure a continuous flow of lubrication during prolonged inverted flight.

A feature of the Leonides engine was the fuel injection system in which the strength of the mixture entering the cylinders was automatically control-led. The possibility of the induction passages icing-up under adverse conditions was considerably reduced by heating them with oil supplied by the lubrication system. Fuel was drawn from the two wing-mounted tanks via a collector tank beneath the floor of the cockpit which housed a booster pump that supplemented the engine-driven pump during starting up by pressurising the injector unit. Movement of the single 'on-off' lever automatically switched on the booster pump. Engine starting was effected by a Coffman cartridge system operated by a lever situated on the floor of the cockpit between the two seats.

A two-stage compressor was mounted on the rear of the engine and supplied air which was stored at a pressure of 450 lb/sq in in a bottle mounted in the fuselage; the compressed air being used to operate the flaps, brakes, engine air-intake and the dual windscreen wipers mounted in the base of each windscreen panel, their speed being regulated by a knob mounted on the central pedestal.

In the cockpit the main flying controls, engine controls, trimming wheels and instrumentation was duplicated. The rudder bars were adjustable over a reach of 6 in made possible by simply pulling a knob – one for each unit – located beneath the instrument panel adjacent to the wall of the cockpit. The control surfaces were moved by a combination of levers and cables; the liberal use of ball-races ensuring a system free of friction and, therefore, light in operation. All control surfaces could be locked on the ground by an integral system operated by a single gated lever in the central control pedestal. This held the throttle controls in a partially closed position which, while permitting the aircraft to be taxied, prevented it becoming air-

borne with the controls locked.

The engine management levers and the trimming controls for the pupil were mounted on the port wall of the cockpit while those for the instructor were housed on the central pedestal. The major flying and engine instruments were duplicated and mounted on panels hinged at their inboard ends to give easy access for the removal of unserviceable units. To prevent damage by vibration, both panels were attached via anti-vibration mountings.

Particular attention was paid to the servicing aspects. For this the airframe was liberally endowed with access panels. Major components could be removed and replaced remarkably quickly, the replacement of a wing which included the removal of the aileron, the flap and its jack, the complete undercarriage leg, the fuel tank and (on the port side) the pitôt

Two refurbished Provosts for the Royal Malayan Air Force. In the background is the M1 motorway (Hunting Aircraft Ltd).

143

Some 3,500 man hours were expended in restoring WW397 (G-BKHP) to flying condition by a crew lead by Flt Lt Crymble who now owns the aircraft (Andrew March).

head took a total of 9¾ man hours. To remove and replace the undercarriage leg – which included the dismantling of the wheel – could be completed in fifty minutes. This was most advantageous for a basic training aircraft which was more than usually subject to accidental damage.

An engineering appraisal made by the Ministry of Supply and issued in March 1951 commented that the simplicity of the design and avoidance of complicated mechanisms contributed to reliability . . . components were easy to change which would reduce the periods of unserviceability resulting from damage or component defects. When the Provost was presented to the Technical Press in May 1951 they were equally as enthusiastic, praising the general construction, the performance and the handling qualities; '*Flight*' reporting in September . . . 'There seems to be no doubt, in fact, that R.A.F. Training Command will receive in their new basic trainers an aircraft most likely among all others to date to find favour with instructors, pupils and ground crews alike. . .'. Enough to bring a glow of satisfaction to the cheeks of any designer!

The statistics of the Provost were: wing span 35 ft 2 in with an aspect ratio of 5.78, a length of 28 ft 8 in, and a height with the tail up of 12 ft 2½ in. The track of the undercarriage was 11 ft 1½ in. The wing had 6° of dihedral measured at the top of the main spar and an angle of incidence at the root of 3° which reduced to 0° at the tip.

Two Provosts, WE503 fitted with the Alvis Leonides and WE522 with the Cheetah were despatched to North Africa where they undertook tropical handling trials at Khartoum between 2 May and 5 July 1951 which entailed a total flying time for both aeroplanes of 211 hr 40 min. In all some 460 Provosts, which included a number armed with machine guns and bombs, were built. They served not only in the Royal Air Force, but in the air forces of Rhodesia, Eire, Burma, Iraq, Sudan and Muscat. It was durng the period of the Sudanese production that the Company suffered its second fatal accident.

Dual instruction was being given by Joe Arnold to a pilot of the Sudanese Air Force in one of their aeroplanes. It was his practice to call the control tower requesting permission to join the circuit. When this had been confirmed Joe would make a low pass, pull up into a loop, roll off the top, make his circuit and land, a manoeuvre he had performed hundreds of times and was, virtually, his trade mark. On this particular day he called the control tower as he normally did and when given the affirmation by the Controller (Bob Easterbrook – later Director of Luton International Airport) he made his usual low pass followed by the loop but instead of rolling out at the top, remained inverted, stalled and spun into the ground killing both occupants instantly. Joe was a popular individual and sadly missed.

In 1953, Percival Aircraft Ltd were given permission to use a Provost as a demonstration aircraft, initially to undertake a sales tour which included Turkey. Bearing the registration G-AMZM, it took off from Luton in July. On its return it did not lose its civil identity and was exhibited at the Farnborough Air Show held in September of the following year. With its responsive controls the Provost was an ideal vehicle in which precise aerobatics could be performed, therefore it was entered in the Lockheed Aerobatic Contest held at Bagington on 20 July 1956. Flying 'MZM, Dick Wheldon made a brave attempt but failed to gain a place.

The Provost remained in service with the RAF for a relatively short period (about 18 years on flying duties) before being replaced by the Jet Provost which, as will be told in the next chapter, completely revolutionised the concept of flying training. As the Provost T.Mk I's were released by the RAF most were purchased by the company and refurbished to meet the demands from foreign air forces who were anxious to employ this remarkable *ab-initio* aircraft on the training of their pilots.

From the hundreds of Provosts built, only a handful have been preserved in static condition by various air museums. As far as is known, only one is still maintained in flying condition. It is a very expensive aircraft to operate and, because of this, is now only flown at air shows where its precise flying qualities continue to delight the visitors.

The aircraft, WW397, first entered the Royal Air Force on 20 September 1954 when it was delivered to No. 12 Maintenance Unit at Kirkbride. Nine days later it arrived at No. 3 Flying Training School, Feltwell where it flew until the school closed 3½ years later after which it was returned to store at No. 27 MU Shawbury, remaining there for eighteen months. On 29 October

1959 it was once again in service, this time with No. 1 FTS, Linton-on-Ouse, but in early 1960 was involved in a flying accident which entailed changing the starboard mainplane.

A year later, in May 1961, it was flown to Shawbury where, once again, it was placed in storage – this time for five years – before being issued to the Central Flying School at Little Rissington on 17 October 1966. After a brief spell at RAF Acklington in July 1967 the Provost then flew in the RAF Coltishall Battle of Britain Display in September 1969. It was again returned to Shawbury where it remained for two months. On 30 October 1969 WW397, by then the last remaining airworthy Provost in the RAF, made its final flight for the Service when it flew to Halton. Here it remained for three years, first serving as a marshalling and ground running training aircraft and finally as an instructional airframe.

In late 1978 a serving officer of the Royal Air Force, Flt Lt M. Crymble, learned that the Provost was available for disposal at Halton. He had first seen the aeroplane while attending his first summer camp at Shawbury as an ATC cadet nine years earlier. He resolved to acquire it and submitted a bid, ostensibly as a 'gate warden', for his station Lyneham. He was successful and WW397 was delivered there in April 1979.

An inspection of the aeroplane when it arrived suggested that the airframe was structurally sound and recovery to flying condition feasible. Fortunately Halton had maintained a complete set of documents and the Air Publications and associated publications were acquired from various sources.

The aircraft was completely stripped down and all 'lifed' components were either replaced or refurbished by an enthusiastic team of NCOs led by Flt Lt Crymble. After some 3,500 man hours had been expended the Provost, resplendent in the colours she had worn when she first entered the Service 29 years previously, made her first flight in the hands of Crymble on 28 May 1983, five years after first arriving at Lyneham. On 1 July of the same year a Permit to Fly was issued.

An application was made to fly WW397 as a service aircraft but, after a lengthy period, this was denied as a matter of MOD policy. The only way that the Provost so painstakingly restored could remain flying was as a civilian aeroplane so Crymble sought permission to buy it. Eventually the sale was agreed and the machine entered the civil register as G-BKHP although it still retained its service livery. Its first public appearance was on 17 July 1983 when it showed its paces at the Badminton Air Day.

CHAPTER 11

THE JET PROVOST

Although the Provost had given the student pilot a head start in achieving his ultimate goal of flying the advanced jet-propelled aircraft then entering service in the Royal Air Force, it was still necessary to convert him to the idiosyncrasies of jet-power. However adept at converting, there was always the real danger that, in an emergency, a pilot would automatically revert to the technique firmly established during his initial training on piston-engined aircraft – often with fatal results.

It is not difficult to understand the problems facing a conventionally trained pilot during his conversion. For instance, a burst of engine power on a propeller-driven aircraft gives an immediate and strong air-flow from the slip-stream over the wings and empennage. This usually delays the stall and restores some form of control response; a technique commonly used in the event of a disastrously heavy landing. Such a technique is not possible with jet-power where, apart from the relatively slow power response, no propeller slip-stream is available.

This had been recognised by Percival Aircraft Ltd who vigorously argued, through Wg Cdr A. N. Kingwill (the Services Liaison Officer) and others, that by introducing jet-power at the *ab initio* stage a student pilot would not be taught practices which could prove fatal later in his flying career. Furthermore, it was postulated, all-through jet training would eliminate the costly conversion stage. As with the introduction of complex propeller-driven aeroplanes at the *ab initio* stage, students capable of flying propeller-driven aircraft but inept at converting to jet-power could be quickly identified and withdrawn from the course at an early stage and not during the conversion period thus reducing unnecessary expenditure of both time and money. This was radical thinking in 1953!

To prove this hypothesis, the Company, under the design code P84, investigated the feasibility of converting the Provost airframe – which had all the attributes of being an outstanding training aircraft – to jet-power and, by doing so, provide a relatively cheap vehicle for that purpose. The power unit selected was the Armstrong Siddeley Viper ASV.5 of 1,640 lb static thrust. It was the 'longlife' version of the expendable engine used in the Australian Jindivik pilotless target aircraft.

The initial design proposals of L. G. Frise (of Frise aileron design) who had been appointed Technical Director and Chief Engineer after the resignation of Arthur Bage in 1948, envisaged the Viper mounted in the nose with the jet efflux discharging under the fuselage. This arrangement was considered to be impracticable and was rejected in favour of a more conventional layout with the power unit mounted in the fuselage

immediately above the wing. To restrain costs, much of the original Provost structure – suitably modified – was utilised.

The original canopy was incorporated in a new nose structure which had two beams built into the bottom to accommodate the nose wheel of the retractable tricycle undercarriage, the power unit was mounted in what was originally the cockpit with large access doors in place of the canopy and the rear end of the fuselage was slightly recontoured to permit the installation of the long jet pipe. A bumper was fitted to the rear of the fuselage to prevent damage in the event of a tail-down landing.

The bifurcated air duct to the engine had two intakes, one on each side of the nose below the canopy. The original empennage was retained but, to compensate for the increased area forward, a dorsal fin was added. The basic Provost wing was modified to accommodate lift spoilers and the retractable main wheel units of the undercarriage, the compression legs being identical to those of the Provost.

The unpainted prototype, without national markings but carrying its service serial number XD674, made a successful maiden flight on 26 June 1954 with Dick Wheldon at the controls. Having proved that the conversion of the airframe to jet power was a viable proposition, a further twelve examples were built to provide aircraft for an evaluation programme conducted by the Royal Air Force.

The programme was in two phases, phase A being undertaken at the Central Flying School; the other at No. 2 Flying School based at Hullavington in Wiltshire.

For the first phase (phase A) three Jet Provost T.Mk I aircraft (as they had been named) were flown intensively by experienced basic and advanced flying instructors for a total of 111 hours during which the handling and general operational qualities of the aeroplanes were evaluated. At the same time the instructors, flying in pairs, gradually assembled a syllabus of instruction appropriate to *ab initio* training on jet-powered aircraft. An evaluation report by the CFS staff at the completion of this phase strongly recommended that the Jet Provost should be adopted.

Using six aircraft serial numbered XD673 to XD678 inclusive, phase B comprised actual flying tuition. The students were not specially selected but happened to be available when the evaluation was being conducted. Some

The prototype Jet Provost T.Mk 1 at the SBAC show held at Farnborough in September 1954 (Shell).

149

The prototype Jet Provost T.Mk 1 enabled the Royal Air Force to become the first to embark on all-jet flying training (Charles E. Brown).

fifty students received instruction of which thirty-five had had no previous flying experience. The rest had received varying amounts of training on piston-engined *ab initio* training aircraft. Only one member of the intake failed to reach the solo standard . . . and he was one of those who had received previous instruction!

On assessing the results it was found that the average time taken to reach the solo stage by students without previous experience was 10 hr 10 min. For the rest, the average was 7 hr 25 min making an average for all students of 9 hr 25 min. This was a remarkable improvement on an average of just over 11 hr taken to achieve a similar level of competance on piston-engined training aircraft. An even more significant fact was that those students trained on the Jet Provost needed no conversion to jet-power.

Perhaps the most striking point in the support of the Jet Provost was made in a report by the CFS Examining Wing which read '. . . the student standard reflects most favourably on the aircraft's suitability as an *ab initio* trainer; compared to the average pupil, the jet-trained student has, in a

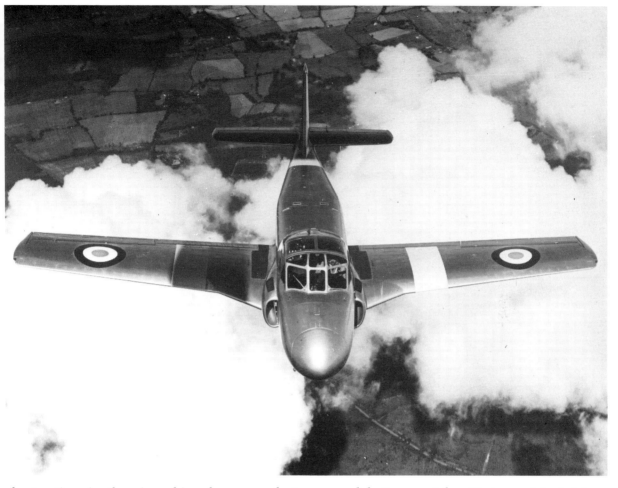

The increased chord of the wing at its root is clearly seen in this shot of the prototype XD674 (Charles E. Brown).

shorter time in the air, achieved a more dexterous and better mental approach to the art of modern flying. His repertoire of aerobatic manoeuvres for example, is more extensive and flown with much more spirit and accuracy. . .'

Following this, the Secretary of State for Air stated in the House of Commons on 8 February 1957 '. . . the evaluation trials have shown that *ab initio* flying training on jet aircraft has definite advantages, and it has therefore been decided to establish this form of training on a larger scale. A production order is being placed for the Jet Provost, which I am satisfied is the best aircraft for the purpose. . .' Thus, nearly three years after the prototype had first flown, the conviction held by Percival Aircraft Ltd that a jet-powered basic trainer was practical and, indeed, an eminently desirable proposition was finally recognised.

Of the twelve Jet Provost T.Mk 1s built, one was used as a demonstration aeroplane allocated the civil registration G-AOBU and granted a Certificate of Airworthiness on 25 May 1955. It was demonstrated at

*Cut-away drawing of the
Hunting Percival Jet Provost
Mk 3 prepared by the
company.*

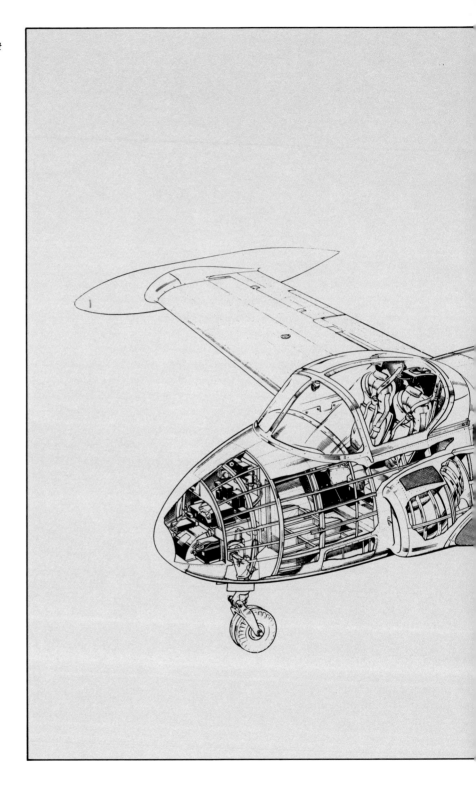

Four of the six Provost T.Mk 1 aircraft of No. 2 Flying School, Hullavington which were used to evaluate the feasibility of ab initio training on jet powered aeroplanes (Central Press).

Blackbushe in the September of the same year and was extensively used at Bitteswell during the following year to undertake development and flight trials on the Armstrong-Siddeley Viper ASV8 engine. In April 1961 it was presented to the Shuttleworth Trust at Old Warden who loaned the aircraft to Loughborough College as an instructional airframe.

During the twenty-odd years in which I was closely associated with aircraft, the centre of gravity was always illusive and never where it was expected to be. The Jet Provost was no exception! To enable the aircraft to be weighed and the actual position of the C of G calculated, it was necessary to tow the machine from its birth-place in the Experimental Hangar to the Main Assembly Shop where the weighbridge was located. During the journey a slight incline had to be negotiated. The operation proceeded without incident until this was reached whereupon the aircraft promptly sat on its tail bumper – much to the consternation of the diminutive engineer stationed in the cockpit to operate the brakes! Fortunately no damage was sustained and the installation of the radio equipment plus a little balast soon restored the C of G to its correct position.

On receipt of the order promised by the Secretary of State for Air, work started in earnest in converting a basic idea into a thoroughly practical

aeroplane. The long-legged undercarriage which tended to 'walk' on rough ground and only installed on the grounds of economy was the first to be replaced. The pneumatic rectraction system efficiently used on previous products gave way to a hydraulic installation. The span of the flaps was increased and with a view to its possible future development the structure was designed to accept the installation of armament with little or no modification. The redesigned aeroplane was designated the Jet Provost T.Mk 2 although the same design code, P84, was retained. Three of the type were built.

The fuselage was constructed in two sections, the front portion, which housed the cockpit and engine bay, terminated at a bulkhead coinciding with the attachment fittings of the rear spar of the wing and the rear part extended to a bulkhead on which were mounted the attachment fittings for the rear spar of the tailplane.

The front half of the fuselage comprised seven sub-assemblies. These were a strong bottom section, two side assemblies, the canopy, decking, engine access panels and a hinged nose cap.

The bottom assembly incorporated two longitudinal beams to take the loads imposed by the nose wheel and form a compartment into which the unit retracted. Further aft were two transverse beams, one for the attachment fittings of the main spar of the wing, the other for the rear subsidiary spar. To these were riveted channel section members to support the floors of the cockpit and engine bay. The assembly was completed by a

One of the twelve Jet Provost T.Mk 1s constructed was allocated the civilian registration G-AOBU and used as a demonstrator (Hunting Percival Aircraft Ltd).

155

After the T.Mk 1 had proved that all-jet basic training was feasible the Jet Provost was redesigned to become more practical. This was the prototype T.Mk 2 (Flight).

metal skin supported on frames and 'Z' section stringers with access panels to allow the inspection of mechanisms and equipment mounted under the floors.

To this assembly were riveted the side assemblies constructed of 'Z' section stringers and frames with light alloy longerons of channel section. The side assemblies were united at their tops by a decking incorporating a windscreen of five optically-flat safety-glass panels. To isolate the two crew members, solid bulkheads were situated at the front and rear of the cockpit area. The one piece sliding canopy was manually operated and ran on two extruded channels attached to the top longerons. These channels were held in situ at their front ends by spring-loaded locating spigots which, if the canopy was jettisoned, lifted the front end into the air stream.

The radio, electrical equipment, batteries and oxygen charging point were mounted in the nose and accessible through a hinged nose cap. The cockpit was entered from either side via a sprung foot pad in each fairing on the engine air intakes and a walkway on the root of each wing which, being in close proximity to the ground, made the use of special ladders – as needed on the Jet Provost T.Mk 1 – unnecessary.

The revised tail end of the prototype T.Mk 2 (Flight).

The rear portion of the fuselage, recontoured to give a better installation of the jet pipe and built in four sections – top, bottom and two sides – was a semi-monocoque structure of frames and 'Z' section stringers covered by a skin of light alloy. A rail attached to the top of the frames supported the front end of the long jet pipe during its assembly and removal; access to the universal joint and seal at the engine being through access panels on both sides of the fuselage. A removable fairing, baffled to prevent the ingress of fuel into the structure, completed the fuselage.

Each wing was built on a single spar with a subsidiary spar to dissipate the loads imposed by the aileron, slotted flap and spoilers. Full depth ribs and formers extended forward from the main spar with a transverse diaphragm supporting two nose riblets between them at the leading edge. The chord at the root was increased by a fairing housing the taxying lamps at the leading edge. The ribs and formers extended aft between the main and subsidiary spars with an auxiliary spar to disperse the loads from the main undercarriage unit and form a compartment which housed the legs when they retracted.

Built into each wing were three lined compartments, two in the leading

The prototype Jet Provost T.Mk 2 shows its paces at the 1955 SBAC show held at Farnborough (Flight).

edge and one aft of the spar outboard of the undercarriage, in which the flexible fuel tanks were installed. The empennage units were struturally identical with those fitted to the piston-engined Provost.

The main wheel units of the undercarriage (fitted with hydraulically-operated disc brakes) retracted inwards and the nose wheel forwards; all units, including the doors, were operated by a single 'through-rod' type hydraulic ram located beneath the floor of the cockpit, hydraulics replacing the former pneumatic system. A cable attached to both ends of the piston rod circumvented a pulley affixed to the nose leg at its pivot point and a pulley assembly mounted on the front face of the spar beam in the fuselage. The pulley assembly comprised three integral pulleys, one large and two small to give differential cable movement. Cables around the smaller pulleys were connected to chains driving sprockets rigidly attached to the main units; the run of the cables being directed via pulleys aft of the spar beam.

The nose wheel doors were operated by push-rods and bell-crank levers and those at the main undercarriage units by push-rods and levers attached to sprockets driven by the undercarriage retraction chains. In an emergency the undercarriage was lowered by compressed air injected into the system on the 'down' side of the ram, the hydraulic pressure on the opposite side being automatically released to prevent a lock. A device was incorporated in the top of the nose leg to ensure that the wheel was centred before retraction.

Some potential customers were being escorted around the factory by a senior member of the Sales Department and they stopped to observe the

158

retraction tests which were in progress. One of the party enquired as to what would happen if the nose wheel was not aligned before it was retracted. Diligently the senior member explained the function of the centring device and, to demonstrate it as action spoke louder than words, gave the nose wheel a kick. Now, the centring unit was designed to operate over an angle of about 45° each side of centre and the enthusiastic kick had pushed it beyond that limit . . . so it stayed there! Unfortunately the undercarriage was retracted simultaneously which did the underside of the

The prototype Jet Provost T.Mk 3. The CFS Examining Wing reported that students trained on the Jet Provost flew with more spirit and accuracy (Flight).

The short undercarriage of the Jet Provost T.Mk 3 improved the ground handling considerably (Hunting Aircraft Ltd).

fuselage a power of good! The senior person had quite a red face and a lot of explaining to do!

The Armstrong-Siddeley Viper ASV8, a single shaft turbo-jet engine with a seven stage axial compressor, an annular combustion chamber and a single-stage turbine, developed 1,750 lb static thrust at 13,800 rpm. It was mounted on two tripods (one on each side of the engine) the main legs of which were secured to fittings bolted to the wing attachment beams and a small tie-strut at the rear restrained the engine in the pitching plane. An accessory gearbox was mounted on the bulkhead at the front of the engine bay and driven by a shaft from the front of the engine. A triangular firewall mounted on the engine adjacent to the combustion chamber coincided with a firewall built into the engine bay. The top portion was dismountable to allow the engine to be removed.

The first Jet Provost T.Mk 2 flew on 1 September 1955. Four prototypes were built, one for the Ministry of Supply (XN177) the remaining three destined to be used as demonstration aeroplanes by the company. During the evaluation trials undertaken at Boscombe Down, some changes were recommended; those of major importance being the replacement of the flat glass panel windscreen by a moulded 'full-view' unit and the installation of Martin-Baker Mk 4 ejection seats. With these incorporated the aircraft was designated the Jet Provost T.Mk 3. The first of the type had its maiden flight on 22 June 1958 but it was to be a year before the first production aircraft were delivered to the Royal Air Force on 26 June 1959.

Following its adoption by the RAF the company energetically spread the gospel of basic training using jet-power. One of the civil demonstration aeroplanes, registered G-AOUS was given a livery of silver with a white top to the fuselage, fin and rudder with a blue flash extending along the fuselage at the change of colour. The registration was in blue outlined with white and the name Jet Provost was painted in red capital lettering outlined in white within the flash at the nose. It was flown to Finland where, in the extreme cold of a Scandinavian winter, it was demonstrated to officers of the Finnish Air Force.

The second civil demonstrator bearing the registration G-AOHD was prepared for a tour of South America and shipped out to Trinidad where it was re-assembled by Mr S. Ashby, one of the Company's service engineers. It was flown by R. N. (Dick) Rumbelow (a test pilot of the Company who was to pilot the aircraft during the tour) in exceptionally hot weather on 21 April 1958. This enabled a check to be made of the performance against the theoretical estimates with which they closely approximated. Seven days later the Jet Provost was flown to Caracus, Venezuela, where it remained until 7 May giving demonstrations to the officers of the Venezuelan Air Force. It then left on a positioning flight to Bogata in Columbia, made in three stages although four were planned, and later demonstrated at the Columbian Air Force at Cali before an enthusiastic audience.

On 23 May, Dick Rumbelow left Cali en-route to Ecuador, his destination being Quito, an airfield at an altitude of 10,000 ft surrounded by the peaks of the Andes. Here the aircraft was demonstrated and flown by a number of officers, including the commanding general, all were most impressed by the performance at such a high altitude. Talara in Northern

The prototype Jet Provost T.Mk 3 becomes airborne at Farnborough during the 1957 SBAC air show (Flight).

The Jet Provost T.Mk 3 was fitted with a moulded 'full-view' windscreen and Martin-Baker Mk 4 ejection seats (Hunting Aircraft Ltd).

Peru was the next port of call, the transit being made in conditions far from ideal over the wildest terrain of the Andes. After a brief stop the flight continued to Lima, the Peruvian Air Force base where, at the request of the PAF, it was proposed to train five students to solo standard – a somewhat formidable task. As the weather at Lima was continually overcast at the time of the visit and the surrounding countryside unfavourable, the experiment was conducted at Chiclayo where conditions were almost perfect for flying training.

Two of the cadets, selected at random, had completed between 40 and 50 hours of primary tuition on piston-engined Stearman aircraft but the remaining three had never flown. Furthermore none of them could speak English! Fortunately Capt Hernandez – the officer seconded to assist Rumbelow – spoke excellent English and was an accomplished Hunter pilot. He was not, however, a qualified instructor. As he had showed prowess in flying the Jet Provost, Dick (who was a qualified RAF instructor) opted to give him a concentrated course, which lasted for five hours, on the art of instructing. It was agreed, because of the language difficulties, that Rumbelow would instruct the partially experienced students while Hernandez took the remaining three novices under his wing. The training using one aircraft and two instructors was completed in a total of 55 flying hours.

All students achieved solo; of the experienced pupils, one took 5 hr 45 min, the other 8 hr, and the rest averaged just over 12 hours. Such concentrated instruction must have placed an enormous strain on both pupils and instructors with a great deal of punishment being absorbed by the aircraft!

On Saturday, 28 June 1958, the Jet Provost was off on its journeys once more, its tour covering Chile, Argentina and Uruguay terminating at Santos Dumont in Brazil on 12 August. For the 8,400 mile tour only a suitcaseful of spares were carried; only one instrument, two navigation lamp filaments, a pair of seals in the brakes, the two tyres of the main wheels, and a flap

The cockpit of a production version of the Jet Provost T.Mk 3 (Hunting Aircraft Ltd).

A small dorsal fin was fitted to the T.Mk 3 version of which XM346 was an example (Hunting Aircraft Ltd).

interconnecting rod needed replacing – an excellent record for an aircraft that had been flown by 123 pilots, had executed more than 630 landings and had flown a total of 178 hours.

Two months after Rumbelow had completed his South American tour in G-AOHD, S. B. Oliver (who had taken over from Dick Wheldon as Chief Pilot) left for Aden flying XN177, the MOS Jet Provost T.Mk 2b, development aircraft flown by the RAF, to undertake a ten week tour of the East. The machine was powered by an Armstrong-Siddeley Viper ASV9 engine, had a full-view moulded windscreen and was fitted with standard production wings which permitted the installation of wing-tip fuel tanks.

From Aden the aeroplane was flown in stages of approximately 350 miles along the coast of the Aden Protectorate to Karachi where the tour was to begin. Principal evaluations were to be made at Mauripur and Risalpur by the Pakistani Air Force and at Jophur by the Indian Air Force. While at Mauripur the engine was changed for the more usual ASV8.

The Indian Air Force requested that a short sample course of basic instruction should be given using their own instructors with two students chosen at random. The two instructors were given an intensive indoctrination and neither pupil had experience of powered flight although both had completed about thirty launches in gliders. One of the chosen students, F. Cdt Iqbal Singh who was instructed by F/L Jatar, achieved solo standard in 9½ hours; the other failed. During this period the Technical Sales Manager, R. J. W. Brown who was accompanying the tour, instructed a team of Indian technicians on the maintenance of the machine.

The third demonstration aeroplane was despatched for evaluation by the Royal Australian Air Force but no orders were forthcoming.

The first of many countries, apart from the RAF, to adopt the Jet Provost was Ceylon. They purchased twelve machines, the aircraft being armed versions designated the Jet Provost T.Mk 51. Two Browning .303 calibre machine guns were mounted at the wing roots, each provided with 600 rounds of ammunition, with eight fragmentation bombs and four rockets carried under the wings. A reflector sight Mk 2 was fitted to the coaming in front of each seat and a G 45B camera gun was mounted in the nose.

Particular attention was paid to armament safety; all armament circuits being rendered safe on the ground and below a pre-determined airspeed, the latter by a contactor fitted in the airspeed indicator system. Additional safety was provided by plugs mounted in the main wheel bays. The feasibility and efficiency of the armament installation was proved by a full-scale trial undertaken in co-operation with the Royal Air Force using the Jet Provost T.Mk 2 serial number XN177.

Ten Jet Provost T.Mk 3 aircraft await delivery at Luton. (Hunting Aircraft Ltd).

An armed version of the Jet Provost T.Mk 3 was used by the Ceylon Air Force (Hunting Aircraft Ltd).

The overall dimensions of all marks, apart from the height over the rudder, varied by a few inches only. To enable comparisons to be made, the statistics for each mark are given in the following table:

	T.Mk 1	T.Mk 2	T.Mk 3
Span	35 ft 5 in	35 ft 2 in	36 ft 11 in
Length	31 ft 11 in	31 ft 10 in	32 ft 5 in
Height	12 ft 8 in	10 ft 2 in	10 ft 2 in
Wing area (Gross)		213 sq ft for all marks	
Wing loading (lb/sq ft)	27.84	27.61	28.99
All-up weight (lb)	5,950	5,900	6,195
Max. speed**	302 mph	330 mph	326 mph
Stalling speed	76 mph	73 mph	75 mph
Rate of climb	2,520 ft/min	2,550 ft/min	2,400 ft/min
Power unit	ASV5	ASV8	ASV8
Static thrust	1,640 lb	1,750 lb	1,750 lb

**The maximum design speed was 437 mph

A Jet Provost T.Mk 4 fitted with an Armstrong-Siddeley Viper ASV201 which developed 2,460 lb static thrust was developed as a private venture using a T.Mk 2 airframe but by that time Hunting Aircraft Ltd had been absorbed into the vast British Aircraft Corporation and is, therefore, beyond the scope of this book.

The Jet Provost and its descendant, the Strikemaster had proved beyond a shadow of a doubt that the theories postulated by Wg Cdr A. N. Kingwill and Hunting Aircraft Ltd were very sound. They had considerably reduced the costs imposed on the flying training budget and had ensured that any cost expended was on pupils of the calibre capable of handling the advanced and expensive aircraft with which the air forces were being equipped. To me, it is very strange that after thirty years of successfully training their student pilots on jet-powered *ab initio* aircraft, the Royal Air Force should, in 1985, contemplate the apparently retrograde step of returning to propeller-driven basic training aircraft – albeit turbine-driven.

The under-wing stores of the Ceylon aircraft comprised four rocket projectiles (seen here with dummy heads) and eight 25 lb fragmentation bombs (Hunting Aircraft Ltd).

*General arrangement
drawing of the Harrier.*

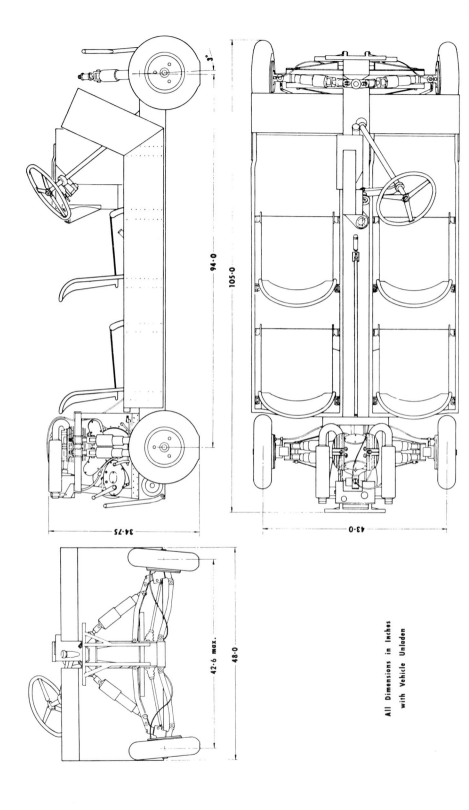

All Dimensions in Inches
with Vehicle Unladen

CHAPTER 12
THE HARRIER

The Second World War had amply demonstrated that mobility was paramount and transport of prime importance. It was obvious that the military commander, during the approach and initial contact with the enemy army, would be faced with logistic time and space problems. These would largely be governed by the availability of wings and wheels, one being used to convey the other to the required destination and in sufficient numbers to ensure the mobility of the forces deployed.

Although large transport aircraft existed at that time which were capable of airlifting standard military vehicles, the space and weight penalty imposed reduced the number of vehicles that could be carried and, therefore, the effectiveness of the operation.

To counter these problems, the Special Weapons Division of Hunting Aircraft Ltd, now Hunting Engineering Ltd, was approached in 1958 with a novel idea for a folding vehicle. Under the direction of Geoffrey Kingslake, the project manager, the idea was developed and a prototype built. Known as the Harrier, it weighed a mere 6¼ cwt and when folded within itself formed a box measuring 1 ft 8 in wide by 2 ft 4 in high and 8 ft 9 in long which occupied a little over 33 cu ft of cargo space compared with the standard ¼ ton truck's 27 cwt which, with the top down and the windscreen lowered, required 370 cu ft of cargo space. Furthermore, the Harrier could be man-handled by its crew without special lifting tackle.

Four members of the team which built the Harrier try to look like authentic soldiers in this publicity photograph with the prototype (Hunting Engineering Ltd).

The Harrier could be manhandled by its crew of four without the use of special equipment and could be made ready for use in one minute (Hunting Engineering Ltd).

The design of the Harrier was both simple and ingenious. It was a robust open four-seat vehicle powered by a 650 cc BSA Type A10 twin-cylinder air-cooled engine mounted at the rear and driving the rear wheels. All four wheels were independently sprung by Armstrong telescopic suspension units carried on pairs of parallel links attached to the chassis member. These links could be folded upward and inward.

The four occupants were carried in hinged panniers locked into position by spring-loaded plungers. Each pannier carried two demountable metal-framed canvas seats and a detachable scuttle at the front to protect the crew from the debris thrown up by the wheels. For aerial transportation the panniers were unlocked and swung upwards and secured together to form a box which was completed by the scuttles which covered the front suspension. During the folding and unfolding operations the chassis was supported on hinged spring-loaded supports.

The main component was a strong steel beam which was 8 ft long with a 6 in square cross-section. This formed a backbone on which all the components were either mounted or hinged. The front wheels were attached by forged wishbones. These gave parallel motion for springing and folding. The suspension units were located between the outer ends of the upper pair of wishbones and a pylon mounted on the forward end of the chassis member.

Rack-and-pinion steering was used; the rack being mounted in a tube within the backbone. It was connected to the front hubs by ball-jointed track-rods which allowed the wheels to be folded without disconnecting the mechanism. The steering column was connected to the steering box through a universal joint and supported by a vertical member (which also carried the fuel tank and the speedometer) via a swinging arm. This permitted the steering wheel to be adjusted for height or be moved upward for folding.

Self balancing brakes, operated by Bowden type cables, were fitted to all wheels and the system was designed to ensure that in a failure at least one pair of brakes remained effective. When the panniers were lowered the foot and hand brake levers connected automatically with the mechanism in the chassis member. The throttle was operated by a conventional accelerator pedal through a Bowden type cable. The clutch control was incorporated with the gear-shift lever mounted between the front seats and on the top of the chassis member. After each gear change the lever returned to the central position. A forward push selected a higher ratio and a backward pull a lower one.

The engine and its motor-cycle type four speed gear box was mounted over the divided rear axle. The drive was by vertical chain from the gearbox to a layshaft mounted within and across the chassis member. From this a chain in the horizontal plane and running in an oil bath drove the centre portion of the rear axle which, to obviate wheel spin on soft or uneven ground, was not fitted with a differential unit. The drive was then transmitted to the rear wheels through two drive-shafts, each having two constant velocity joints, the outer pair having splines to permit the disconnection of the shafts during the folding operations.

An oil tank was mounted on the rear of the engine mounting structure. This comprised two vertical channel members, one at the front of the engine and the other at the back, bolted to the chassis member with 'L' section beams at their tops connected by two fore-and-aft tubes welded to their extremities. The tubes carried adjustable fittings to which the rear suspension units were attached.

The rear suspension was similar in design to that used at the front except that the wishbones were attached to the chassis member through a forged fitting with hinge pins at the front; the rear attachment was by pins which were withdrawn by a lever mechanism mounted within the backbone. To dissipate the load imposed by the engine, the rear suspension was fitted with four suspension units, two on each side.

An electric fuel pump and lighting was fitted, the power being supplied by a battery charged through a voltage regulator by an engine-driven generator.

The Harrier could be folded or unfolded by its crew in less than a

One of the six prototype Harriers supplied for evaluation fitted with larger wheels and mud-guards (Hunting Engineering Ltd).

minute. To prepare it for use from the folded condition, the vehicle was hoisted on to the stands and the two scuttle panels removed. The rear wheels were then lowered and turned through right-angles and the splined ends of the drive-shafts coupled to the wheels. The complete assembly was then locked in position by moving the locking lever upwards. Next, the lower ends of the suspension units, two on each side, were aligned with holes in the upper wishbone members and secured by quick-release pins.

The front wheels were then lowered, the pylon assembly rotated through 90° and the lower ends of the suspension units aligned with the holes in the upper front wishbone members. These too were secured by quick-release pins. Next the panniers were released and lowered where they were locked in the down position; the seat frames were inserted in their mounting channels and the scuttle panels erected. Finally the steering wheel was swung into position and locked by a star-wheel.

When I first inspected the Harrier I had the impression that the small wheels, only 1 ft 4 in diameter over the tyres, would be inadequate for cross-country running and its use would be restricted to fairly smooth terrain, but this was soon dispelled by Geoff in a spectacular demonstration of the

Harrier's cross-country ability – and most hair-raising it was! The top speed was about 50 mph but, perched in the panniers on canvas seats a few inches above the ground with no form of constraint (seat belts were then not a legal requirement) and with the engine bellowing away through two short exhaust pipes few inches from the ears, it seemed more like 150 mph!

When driven over rough terrain, the smooth, flat underside acted as a sledge which slid over the obstacles until traction was regained. If, however, traction was lost – which it never was when I was on board – the crew simply lifted it off the obstruction and carried on! To be fully effective a high speed had to be maintained and it was most disturbing to leave a metalled road with no reduction in speed and career across a rubbish tip; a demonstration fiendishly relished by Kingslake!

Kingslake also claimed that the Harrier was amphibious, the panniers would act as bouyancy chambers, the rear wheels as paddles and the front ones as rudders – but he never had the facilities or was allowed to prove this theory!

The Army was most impressed with the idea and ordered six prototype vehicles for evaluation purposes. They also considered that the small wheels would be detrimental to the cross-country performance and insisted that larger wheels with mud-guards should be fitted. This entailed a detail re-design and the opportunity was taken to incorporate a number of refinements but, to me, the performance of the later Harriers were not so good as the original version.

By the time the evaluation had been completed it was obvious that the transport aircraft entering the service would be large enough to carry vehicles of conventional design and in reasonable quantities. This nullified the need for the Harrier and no further orders were forthcoming.

One Harrier still exists and is on display in the Museum of Army Transport at Flemingate, Beverley, North Humberside. According to the museum's director, Col C. E. (Teddy) Petter, this sole surviving Harrier is still very mobile and, to quote from a letter received from him on 17 July 1984, '. . . we have it on the road and very much in use by our Mobile Display team. This means that the vehicle is taken around mainly local galas and fetes and its 'boxable' capability is demonstrated rather like the Earls Court Gun Drill.'

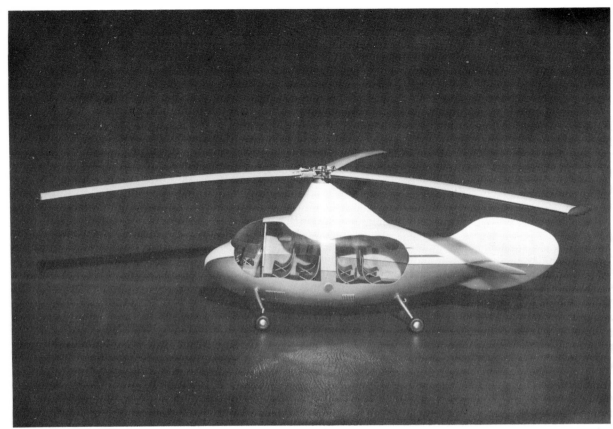

A model of the P74 helicopter in its original form with a large fin and rudder aimed at using the down-wash from the rotor blades for yaw control (Percival Aircraft Ltd).

CHAPTER 13

THE UNFORTUNATE P74 AND ITS VARIANTS

By 1950 the factory was very busy producing the Jet Provost and Pembroke but rotary-wing aircraft appeared to be the flying machines of the future. The principles of the helicopter had been outlined in the fifteenth century by Leonardo Da Vinci but some five centuries were to pass before the technology of the twentieth century permitted those principles to be applied.

It was not until the World War of 1914–1918 that helicopters were first flown – in Germany – albeit in the captive mode. But it was not until 18 April 1925 at Issy-les-Moulineaux in France that a helicopter designed by the Marquis de Pescara managed to fly, more or less under control, for a distance approaching one kilometer. During this period between the two world wars several helicopters had been designed and successfully flown and in doing so had established a number of international records. However, in modern parlance, they were all purely research aircraft and limited in their application. However all the designs had one common denominator – they were all complicated!

In an attempt to overcome this complexity caused by the mechanically-driven rotor blades, the idea of propelling them by a power source at their tips seemed very attractive. The first recorded use of this system was in France in 1926 on an aircraft known as the Isacco Heliogyre. It had a rotor assembly comprising four blades driven by small engines of 33 hp mounted on each tip with a further 50 hp engine providing the forward thrust. Although the idea was very simple and in spite of further experiments with the system conducted in England in 1930 using engines of greater power, the device was not a success.

It took a second world war and the ingenuity of Igor Sikorsky to boost the development of the helicopter into a useful and practical flying machine. His design, the R-4B, first flew in America in 1942 and amply demonstrated that the helicopter had much potential. After the cessation of hostilities development surged ahead. A number of designs were built, mostly in America, which explored the possibilities of the attractive tip-driven rotor blade, some with limited success.

In pursuance of this scheme the newly-formed Helicopter Division of the company under the direction of the Technical Director L. G. Frise (who had replaced Arthur Bage when he resigned in 1949) undertook a comprehensive study into the use of gas-turbines to achieve greater simplicity. L. G. had a 'thing' about helicopters and his large office had a display case down one side full of models of this form of machine. The investigation he conducted examined every possible method of propulsion

The rotor assembly about to be test run in the pit (Hunting Engineering Ltd).

that was available at the time.

Based on the work carried out in Austria during the second world war by an engineer named Dublof in which gas supplied by a generator was used at a relatively low temperature (but high in volume), the conclusion was reached that the simplest solution would be to design a special gas producing plant and to direct the entire product of combustion through the blades and out through jets at their tips.

Two important advantages were claimed for the system, the first being that a compact overall configuration would result from the jet-drive at the rotor tips and that an anti-torque device as required on helicopters of conventional design with mechanically-driven rotor blades would not be needed. Such a design would enable the extremities of the fuselage to be kept within the swept area of a single lifting rotor.

The second advantage claimed was that a simple gas drive to the rotor blades would avoid the need for complex mechanical couplings (shafts, gearboxes etc.) and would thus eliminate the vibration and fatigue problems associated with such items. It was also claimed that the replacement of the moving parts used in shaft-driven rotors by static equivalents (i.e. the gas-duct system) would reduce complexity and, therefore, the initial costs together with the subsequent maintenance charges. (Such claims had been postulated by former avocates of tip-driven rotor systems.)

Another feature of the proposed design was the rotor hub. This was tilting and free to rotate on the true rotor axis for any condition of flight; thus the need for drag hinges was eliminated and the aerodynamic vibrations usually associated with conventionally-driven rotors when in forward flight was reduced. It was acknowledged that many design problems had to be surmounted but the simplification of a system that had no moving parts (except the rotor blades) and therefore required no lubrication, suffered no wear or was subjected to fatigue limitations would more than offset these.

Resulting from these investigations a research helicopter was proposed and allocated the design code P74. The Ministry of Supply had indicated that they were interested in the project and had placed an order with D. Napier and Son for the development of a small gas-generator to be known as the Orynx N.Or.1. In November 1951 the two companies working as a team continued the investigations and made the design calculations. As a result, early in 1952 Hunting Percival Aircraft Ltd were awarded a contract, 6/Aircraft/7054/CB.8(a), for the design and manufacture of a flying test-bed for the jet-driven rotor system using the Orynx gas-generating engine.

Under the control of John Wooton the Chief Project Engineer supported

Two Napier Orynx gas-generator engines with an extra cold stage were slung side-by-side beneath the cabin (Flight).

The initial engine test runs were made without the main and tail rotors (Hunting Percival Aircraft Ltd).

by a team comprising Charles Bradbury and Dennis Moore as Principle Designers with two Polish gentlemen, Marion Lesniak and Ivan Tustanowsky as aerodynamist and thermodynamist respectively, the detail design of the P74 commenced. In its initial form the fuselage incorporated a large fin with an inclined hinge rudder aimed at using the down-wash for yaw control. This, together with the four-wheeled undercarriage, gave the aeroplane the appearance of a tadpole prior to its final evolution into a frog, however it was becoming pretty obvious that the fin would be insufficient to provide the necessary yaw control so, to avoid any possible difficulty during the flight test programme (and although it demolished part of the argument that the mechanics were simple) it was replaced by a tail rotor.

The fuselage, mounted on four tortionally-sprung undercarriage legs, the front pair of which were fully orientatable, was of oval cross-section and constructed of frames and stringers covered by a skin of light alloy. A crew of two was accommodated in the nose in side-by-side seating beneath a large moulded 'Perspex' canopy fitted with two large opening panels, one on each side. The compartment was separated from that of the passengers by a bulkhead in which was a door.

In front of the crew's seats and on the centre-line of the aircraft was a pedestal on which was mounted the engine management levers, the 'trim' wheels, fuel control levers and the gas bypass levers. Above this was a small sub-instrument panel carrying the rev. counters and warning lamps etc. The main instrument panel was ranged on either side of the pedestal, the portion on the right-hand side (when viewed from the seats) mounting the flying instruments and that opposite the instrumentation for monitoring the gas generating system.

Dual controls were fitted with the yaw controlled by pedals and the cyclic pitch by conventionally-placed control columns. Collective pitch was applied by two levers, one for each pilot, attached to a short operating tube mounted in the transverse plane immediately above the control pedestal. These levers could be locked by rotating a knob situated at the top of the pedestal.

The passengers' cabin, accessible through a large door at the rear on the port side, was divided into two saloons by a compartment on both sides housing the gas transportation ducts. At each seat position there was an oval window with a further window situated on the starboard side opposite the entrance door. The four passengers in the forward saloon faced to the front while those in the rear one faced aft. In the event the seats were never fitted as the cabin housed a mass of instrumentation. At the rear of the cabin a further bulkhead was fitted with a door through which access could be gained to the structure of the rear fuselage.

The two Napier Orynx gas-generator engines with an extra cold stage were slung side-by-side in bipod mountings beneath the floor of the cabin and were accessible through generously proportioned detachable panels on each side. Air was drawn through eight oval orifices pierced in the skin of the fuselage immediately forward of the engine compartment. Fuel was carried in tanks located beneath the cabin floor forward and aft of the engine

The cockpit showing the collective pitch levers and the conventionally placed cyclic pitch levers. Yaw was controlled by the foot pedals. The flying instruments were mounted on the right hand panel (as viewed) and that on the left hand accommodated the monitoring instrumentation for the gas generating system (Flight).

compartment with filler necks on the starboard side.

The gas generated by the engines, after being mixed with cold air, was transported through two ducts, one from each unit, which ran vertically up the sides of the cabin and converged above the ceiling. From there it passed to the hollow rotor hub (fitted with gas-tight flexible bellows) to ducts within the rotor blades and thence to the tips where it was discharged.

A remotely-controlled valve, operated by the levers on the pedestal in the cockpit, was situated at the base of each vertical duct within the fuselage. These permitted the engines to be run at full power during start-up, the residual gas being discharged in a hazardous position at chest height through orifices in the sides of the fuselage. The valves gradually closed as the revolutions of the rotor increased until all the gases were being directed through the blade ducts. When normal operating speed had been reached the valves then partially opened to prevent the rotors over speeding. In the event of an engine failure these valves ensured that a reverse flow did not occur through the inoperative unit.

This hazardous position of the valves was amply demonstrated during the early runs according to George Allen, a member of the Napier Service Department at Acton Vale but on secondment to Luton. From his account the proceedings would have done credit to the best of the Keystone Cops!

According to his narrative, the engines were started and the by-pass valves in the exhaust system huffed and puffed. An enthusiastic fireman got too close to them and had his whiskers singed. Forthwith, he was rushed off to hospital for treatment; the fire engine being used as a make-shift ambulance. Unfortunately the appliance was still attached via a hose to the hydrant. As the fire engine rushed off on its mission of mercy the hose stretched until it finally broke! The onlookers, it seems, didn't know whether to laugh or cry.

The three non-feathering rotor blades, each fitted with three ducts, were constructed from stainless steel and a decisive factor in their design was the shape and total cross-sectional area of these ducts. This determined the aerofoil section. The ducts chosen were about 5 or 6 inches in diameter and of circular cross-section which resulted in a thick aerofoil section. Although this gave a high aerodynamic drag factor it was considered that it would be effectively off-set by lower internal frictional losses in the gas flow. To minimize the drag factor a laminar flow aerofoil of NACA 664422.5 section was used which had a 22.5% thickness to chord ratio and produced laminar flow properties over 50% of its chord.

However, the low-drag incidence was insufficient to apply over the complete flight envelope and the aerodynamic characteristics of laminar flow sections – particularly the pitching moment as to a function of incidence – did not lend themselves to the normal cyclic pitch variation so the blades were of fixed pitch and the camber changed by full-span ailerons to provide the necessary cyclic variations. The ailerons were segmented and operated by levers controlled by steel ribbons held in tension by centrifugal forces acting upon weights at their outer ends. To compensate for a

reduction in the mass flow of gas in the event of one of the engines failing, variable-area nozzles of clam-shell design were fitted to the tips of the rotor blades.

The blades were 55 ft in diameter with a chord of 27.57 in and fabricated from stainless steel. They were of monocoque construction with a spar at the trailing edge to dissipate the loads imposed by the ailerons. The ribs were closely spaced at about 6 inches pitch and covered by a one-piece skin with additional reinforcing skins over the highly-stressed root area. This introduced some very complex spot-welding techniques. A special jig was built to ensure that the welding mandrils were always at right-angles to the surface throughout the camber to achieve a smooth finish which is essential in a laminar flow aerofoil. As the spot-welding, due to the one-piece skin, was executed blind, the equipment (including the operator) rode on a carriage running on a tube approximately 2 ft in diameter. The carriage was accurately locked at each rib station.

The design of a static rig to test the complete rotor system had been started toward the end of 1951 and in just over two years, in July 1954, it had been completed and fully furnished. The walls of the pit, formed by dumping the spoil around the periphery during excavation, was designed to slope at such an angle that the down-draught from the rotor under test was deflected outward and upward to minimize the recirculation of the air. The level of the rotor under test was well below that of the rim to reduce the noise level and the hazzard in the event of a failure. An armoured control room was sunk into the wall of the pit.

The P74 helicopter, less the tail rotor, is seen here tethered on Luton Airport during one of the many attempts to get it airborne (Hunting Engineering Ltd).

In parallel with the early work on the rotor test pit, an experiment was designed to compare the laminar flow characteristics of the proposed NACA 664422.5 and 663318 aerofoil sections. This experiment was mounted in the pit prior to the installation of the tower. For reasons of economy a Sikorsky R4B helicopter, a number of which had been purchased from a local scrap yard, was mounted on special supports which gave freedom of movement in the horizontal plane. The tortional freedom was restrained by a torque measuring device attached to the rear of the fuselage, the tail rotor having been removed. This measured the drag of the specimen under test. These were fabricated from ply and balsa wood with a coating of china-clay matt dope which, when wetted with kerosene, clearly showed any turbulence. For the test the 48 inch long section, fitted with a full-span aileron, was mounted on a 'whirling arm' which replaced the rotor blades.

The procedure for putting the contraption into motion was – to say the least – 'hairy' according to a report written in March 1954. The operation required the services of at least three persons. After the engine had been started normally, the arm was rotated by hand to overcome the inertia. The throttle was then slowly opened and the clutch carefully engaged; an operation performed by two persons stationed in the cockpit – one for each control – to ensure that the operation of the levers was smooth and progressive. When the clutch was fully engaged and the rig running smoothly the crew retired to the safety of the control cabin to perform the test. Only the NACA 66422.5 section was tested as the clutch burned out due to the heavy loads imposed.

When the design of the Orynx was first initiated, due consideration had to be given to the operating conditions of the ducting within the blades. This limited the temperature of the exhaust from the engine. As the motive power used in the static rig was provided by a Rolls-Royce Derwent engine which operated at a much higher temperature, its exhaust was fed into a duct of circular cross-section into which water was injected to achieve the stipulated temperature conditions and to keep the exhaust with the gas-flow parameters, a simple variable-area nozzle was fitted which enabled surplus gas (i.e. that not ducted to the rotor tips) to be discharged through a pipe and clear of the pit.

Early in 1953 air-flow tests were conducted in a Government establishment using a half-scale model of the proposed rotor hub gas duct. It was discovered that the flow of gas was very much restricted. The need for greatly increased duct cross-sections led to a complete re-design of the rotor hub system. This re-design work was undertaken by the Senior Mechanical Designer, Geoffrey Dollimore, later Chairman of Hunting Engineering Ltd. The necessarily larger hub dimensions led to the use of fabricated high strength stainless steel structures in place of the former proposals to use a cast unit. The re-design increased the development programme by about a year.

The tests continued and during one of the runs the windmilling of the blades after the power had been shut off created a vacuum over the blade tips which caused the .005 in thick ducting within the blade to implode. However, the problems encountered were of a minor nature and a total of 50 hours running time was achieved in a shorter elapsed time than was normal in the industry.

Although the tests had proved that the rotor system worked, there was a strong feeling within the design team that the choice of a laminar flow aerofoil was unwise. To work efficiently such a section had to be precisely made and clinically clean. It was possible to meet the first requirement but not the second. Helicopters usually operate, for most of their working lives, at low altitudes and therefore in the 'fly belt' where the insects would impact on the leading edge and quickly destroy the laminar flow properties.

With this in mind, Charles Bradbury and Geoffrey Dollimore assisted by two other members of the team working on a part-time basis, produced schemes using the best elements of the P74 but employing conventional cyclic pitch and 'normal' aerofoil section. This was allocated the design code P104.

Based on this study a further design study, the P105, was produced in which the main rotor assembly and gas generating units were arranged to form a compact unit complete with an auxiliary gearbox and tail rotor coupling. It was envisaged that the fuselage would be a separate unit on to which the rotor/gas generating system would be mounted; an arrangement that allowed greater freedom in the design and particularly important in view of the various roles envisaged.

In an optimistic brochure issued by the company in August, 1955 (to quote) '. . . based on the measured efficiency of the gas-drive system which has been tested on the Hunting Percival P74 research helicopter, coupled with various improvements which enable full advantage to be taken of the inherent simplicity of the tip-driven rotor. . .', two of the possible roles were described together with a detailed description of the gas-generating system.

Couched in very positive terms, the description stated that the rotor was 63 ft in diameter and had three blades constructed of stainless steel with light alloy tail fairings and that the cast stainless steel hub structure was mounted on two taper-roller bearings and accommodated the blade flapping bearings of the plain type . . . which required no lubrication.'

An artist's impression depicted the two gas-generating units mounted at the tips of a short stub-wing to form a single unit with the rotor support structure together with the auxiliary gearbox, tail rotor drive-shaft and the oil system enclosed within a light alloy fairing. One of the roles described was a general-purpose helicopter, the other an aerial crane.

Although the P74 was designed to have a simple rotor system, there was considerable argument within the team as to whether the controls should be power assisted. Theoretical calculations indicated the need for power on the collective pitch system but not on the cyclic as in theory a rotor of any size could be made to operate without power assistance – although this was not advocated by the senior members of the design team.

Initial representation to L. G. Frise to incorporate power assistance was rejected on the grounds that complexity would be increased and the whole concept that the system was simple would be destroyed. Fred Pollicutt had joined the company as Chief Designer about this time and a fresh review of the possible problem was made. After much discussion a compromise was reached. Power assistance would be fitted − but to the collective pitch only.

In May 1956, the aircraft finished in silver overall with national markings and bearing the serial number XK889, was rolled out and prepared for the initial engine runs minus the rotor assembly. When these had been successfully completed the blade assembly was installed and the machine moved on to the aerodrome to begin tethered flight tests. These were undertaken by Wilfrid Gellatly, then at the A&AEE Boscombe Down but later Chief Pilot of Westland Helicopters Ltd, assisted by an RNAS pilot whose name has unfortunately been forgotten.

When flight was attempted all was not as expected. It was evident that power assistance on the cyclic pitch system was essential. Although both pilots' struggled manfully on a number of attempts, the controls would not budge. Furthermore, the thick aerofoil section created too much drag and there was insufficient power to overcome it − in other words it was underpowered − so the aeroplane emulated that well-known New Zealand bird, the Kiwi, and stayed firmly on the ground.

Drastic action was needed if the machine was to fly. The first aim was to overcome the resistance in the cyclic pitch system. The simplest method was to fit hydraulic rams, but as there was insufficient space on the airframe it was proposed that these should be fitted externally and operated from the ground. To overcome the power problem it was proposed to update the machine to a Mark II version by fitting a more powerful Rolls-Royce RB108 engine. A report was produced outlining the latter and it included a design study (allocated the design code P113) in which the re-designed rotor system was incorporated in addition to the Rolls-Royce RB108.

Unfortunately the sands of time were running out. The Ministry of Supply, seeking a rationalization of the helicopter industry, carried out an investigation and came to the conclusion that there were too many fingers in the pie. As a result all contracts were cancelled leaving Bristol Helicopters Ltd the responsibility for the design and Westland Helicopters Ltd the manufacture of all rotary-wing aircraft carrying a Government subsidy. The final proposals submitted by the company which would, most probably, have proved that the system was viable were rejected and on instructions from the MOS the P74 was ignominiously cut up and sold for scrap.

CHAPTER 14
FINALE

From 1954 the company had operated under the name Hunting Percival Aircraft Ltd and in 1956 had opened a branch office in Toronto, Canada but in 1957 all links with the founder were severed when the name Percival was dropped and the title of Hunting Aircraft Ltd was adopted. At about the same time the newly-named company participated with the Fairey Aviation Company and de Havilland Holdings Ltd in the formation of a consortium which was known as the Aircraft Manufacturing Company. This was formed primarily to produce the DH121 Trident which had been chosen by British European Airways Ltd as a replacement for their ageing Viscount aircraft.

During the same period Hunting Aircraft Ltd had conducted an intensive investigation into the possible need for a short-haul jet-powered airliner. This entailed members of the design team travelling on a number of scheduled flights operated by various airlines and in a variety of aircraft; the aim being to establish the good and bad features of each machine. From the information gathered from the subsequent reports written by the participants the design criterior was gradually evolved under the design code P107.

The final proposal was for a low-wing monoplane powered by two Bristol Orpheus B.Or.3 engines mounted at the rear of the fuselage. The wing span was 80 ft 10 in, the overall length 81 ft 9 in, and the height over the rudder was 24 ft. The wing was swept back at 20° − measured at the 25% chord line − and its gross area was 800 sq ft with a chord at the root of 14 ft 9 in which reduced to 5 ft 3 in at the tip. The thickness ratio was 13% and 10% respectively. The all-up weight was 44,800 lb which would have given a wing loading of 56 lb/sq ft.

The total area of the fin and rudder was 97.5 sq ft, the tailplane and elevator 172.36 sq ft; this unit being mounted on the fin at about a third of its height.

The main units of the tricycle undercarriage, each fitted with four wheels on a common axle, retracted backwards into the wing root and had a track of 12 ft. The steerable nose wheel unit, fitted with twin wheels, was mounted on the centre-line of the aeroplane beneath the pilots' cockpit and was 31 ft in front of the main wheel units.

The fuselage of circular cross-section provided accommodation for a crew of four (plus the cabin crew) and between 48 and 56 passengers dependent upon the stage length. The pressurised cabin was 57 ft in length, was 9 ft wide with a headroom of 6 ft 3 in throughout the entire length. Access to the cabin was through two doors, one at the front, the other at the

An artists' impression (by the author) of the Hunting 107 which was developed into the BAC111 (Hunting Aircraft Ltd).

rear, both being on the port side. Double seats, each adjacent to the window, were fitted on both sides of the cabin with a central gang-way 1 ft 5 in wide at the arm rests. A standard feature of all the cabin layouts was the 135 cu ft luggage compartment and toilet situated at the rear of the cabin. Further baggage could be stowed in a 183 cu ft hold situated beneath the cabin floor.

To sell the design to interested parties a very comprehensive brochure was produced which, on the insistance of Mr Thoms who was in charge of the project design team, included detailed perspective cut-away drawings of each major component. Fortunately my team were all experienced in the design and manufacture of aircraft, a number being ex-apprentices or past members of the Royal Air Force, so this caused no outstanding problems. However, a last minute requirement, made two days before the document

was to be 'put to bed', was for a three-quarter cut-away drawing of the complete aeroplane!

The H126 under construction. To gain access to the structure and equipment, inspection panels were liberally used (Hunting Aircraft Ltd).

I was reluctant to accept this challenge but one of my senior and most experienced illustrators, Peter Clifford, had different ideas! Working at home to avoid the distraction that would have inevitably occurred at the office, Peter worked through the night and the following day – with a constant supply of hot black coffee – and completed the task a few hours before the dead-line! When the company was absorbed into the British Aircraft Corporation (as it was then known) the design was developed into the BAC 111 and proved to be a successful airliner.

Fred Pollicutt, who had joined the company in 1953, was appointed Chief Designer and Technical Director in 1956 when L. G. Frise resigned the post. Under his control the H126 was built and was to be the last aeroplane to be designed at Luton. It was a research aircraft built under a Ministry of Aviation contract to investigate the principle of lift augmentation using a jet flap.

It was a high-wing monoplane powered by a single Bristol Siddeley Orpheus engine. The fuselage was of oval cross-section with a conventional structure of light alloy frames and stringers covered by a skin of light alloy. The engine was buried within the deep fuselage and breathed through a large orifice in the nose. The single pilot was accommodated in a cockpit

The empennage was fitted as a complete assembly (Hunting Aircraft Ltd).

with a one-piece sliding canopy above the intake ducting which positioned him quite a distance from the ground.

Efflux from the engine was ducted through the wing and discharged as a thin sheet of gas from the trailing edge to produce both lift and thrust over full span flaps, the outer ends of which were used as ailerons. To augment the thrust provided by this means, two direct-thrust nozzles were positioned low down on both sides of the fuselage aft of the wing. Further smaller nozzles were situated, one at the extreme tail which was used for the pitch-trim and two further nozzles, one on each side of the fuselage beneath the leading edge of the fin, for yaw control.

Longitudinal control and stability was provided by a conventional fin and rudder supplemented by a dorsal fin. The tailplane and elevator were mounted high on the fin which also housed an anti-span parachute in a compartment built into its top.

The high-aspect wing with a thick aerofoil section was built in two sections and braced by single struts from the rear spar, at about half span, to the bottom of the fuselage. The full span flap hinged about brackets bolted

DANGER – JET EXHAUST

XN714

to the bottom surface of the wing and were hydraulically-operated by rams also below the lower surface of the wing and covered by blister fairings.

The tricycle undercarriage was fixed; the single-wheel main units being supported by compression legs attached to the fuselage slightly below the wing and braced by 'V' struts at the bottom of the fuselage. The orientatable nose-wheel unit carried twin wheels and comprised a compression leg braced by a single strut at the rear to absorb the landing loads.

The aeroplane, finished in silver overall with a black anti-dazzle panel on top of the fuselage in front of the windscreen and carrying national markings with the serial number XN714, was transported by road to the Royal Aircraft Establishment at Bedford where it made its first flight during the afternoon of 26 March 1963. The flight was of 20 minutes duration and undertaken by S. B. Oliver who was the Chief Test Pilot of Hunting Aircraft. He expressed complete satisfaction with the initial flight which amply demonstrated the aeroplane's ability to take-off and land at much lower speeds.

The Government in power during the 1950s and early 1960s advocated the amalgamation of small aircraft companies into one or two large organisations which, they considered, would be much more efficient. The Hunting Group had always been independent, making their own decision to achieve their own objectives, but faced with veiled threats that Government contracts would only be placed with the larger organisations,

In this view the pitch-trim nozzle can be seen at the extreme end of the fuselage together with port yaw nozzle beneath the leading edge of the fin. An anti-spin parachute was fitted in the top of the fin (Hunting Aircraft Ltd).

Gas produced by the engine was ducted through the wing and ejected over full span flaps; the outer sections also doubled as ailerons (Hunting Aircraft Ltd).

The last aeroplane to be designed at Luton was the H126. It was a purely research aircraft to investigate the jet flap principle (Hunting Aircraft Ltd).

only one option remained. Arrangements were made for the British Aircraft Corporation to acquire a controlling interest. For a short time Sir Percy continued to serve as Chairman but eventually he resigned, the post being taken by Sir George Edwards, CBE, BSc, Hon FRAeS who had been appointed vice-chairman at the time of the take-over.

And so, from September 1960, a company that had done much in the field of aircraft design and manufacture over a span of 28 years virtually ceased to exist. The manufacture of the Jet Provost, although continued for a short period at Luton, was transferred to the Preston Division of the British Aircraft Corporation, the staff dispersed and the premises sold to Vauxhall Motors limited. Eventually the site was sold to property developers.

Almost fifty years after a small but not insignificant Percival Aircraft Company became the first residents at an infant Luton Airport, only a road bearing the name Percival Way on the now busy Luton International Airport provides evidence that the company ever existed. Now nothing remains. In 1986 all the buildings were razed to the ground and the 21 acre site earmarked for industrial development.

Only one H126 research aircraft was built and was powered by a single Bristol Siddeley Orpheus engine (Hunting Aircraft Ltd).

APPENDIX:

Scale drawings of Major
Percival and Hunting Percival
designs are reproduced from
company archives on the
following pages

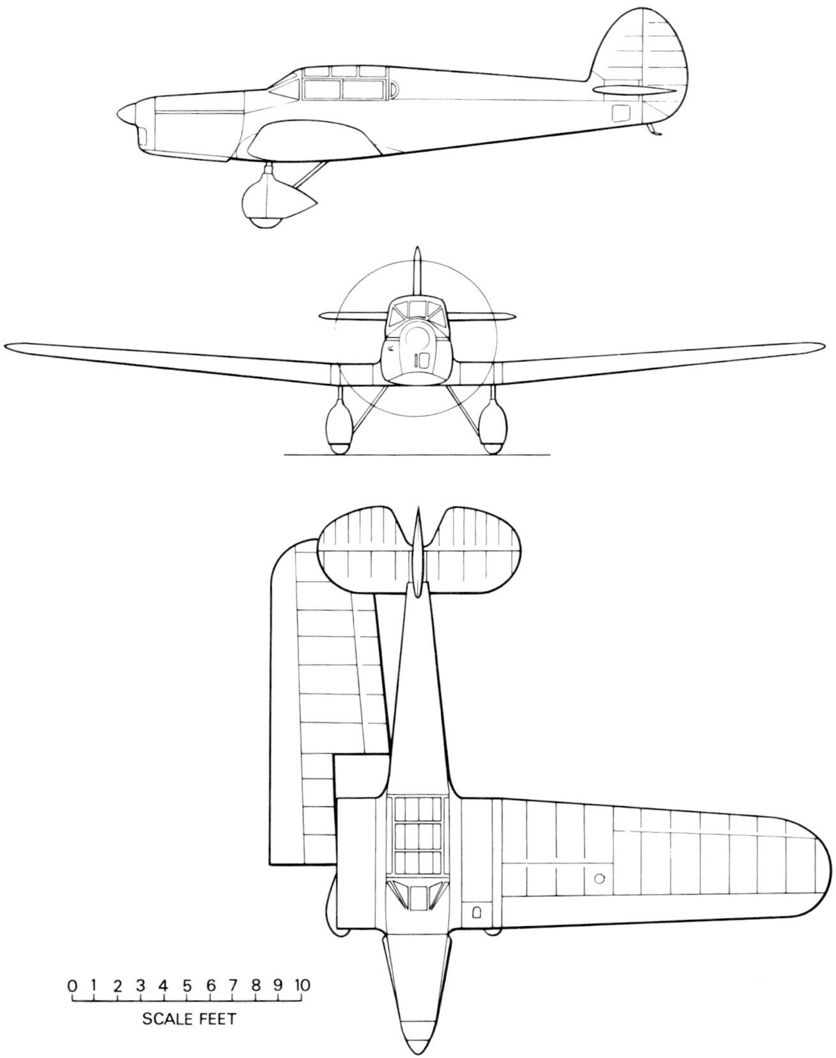

Vega Gull I

G-AFIE

Gull

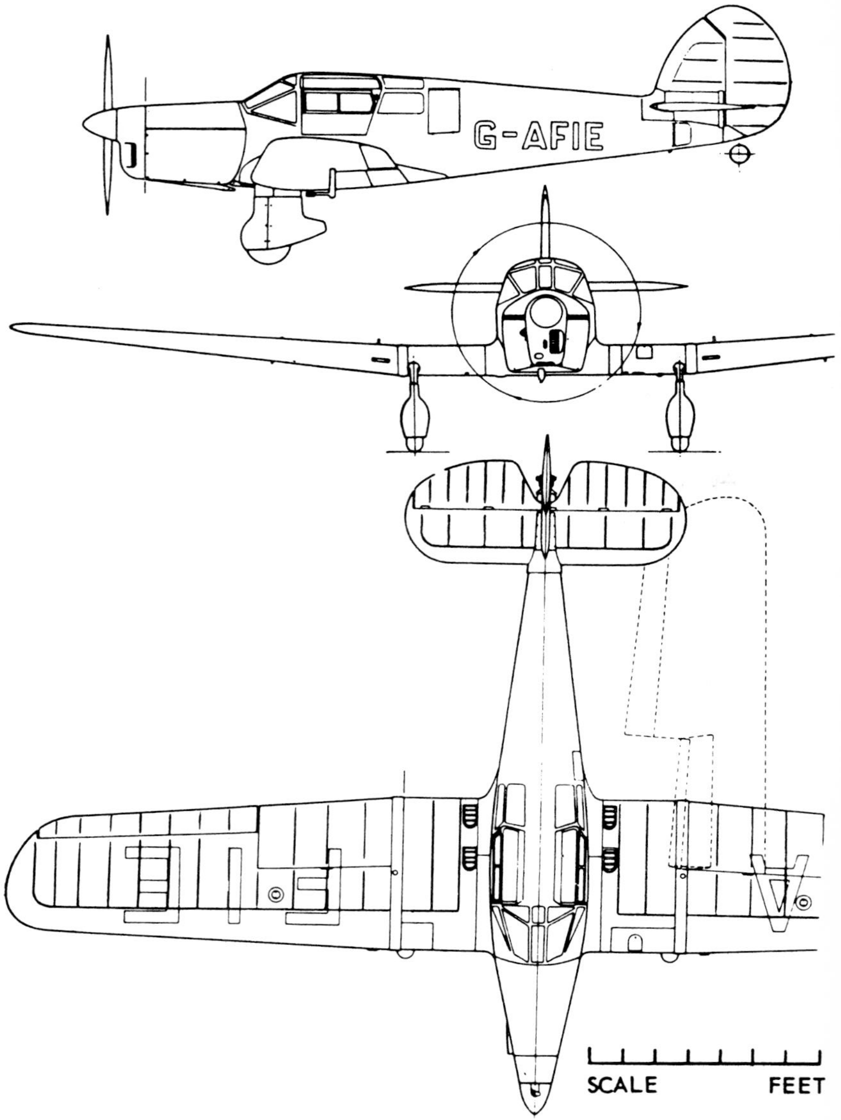

Q.6

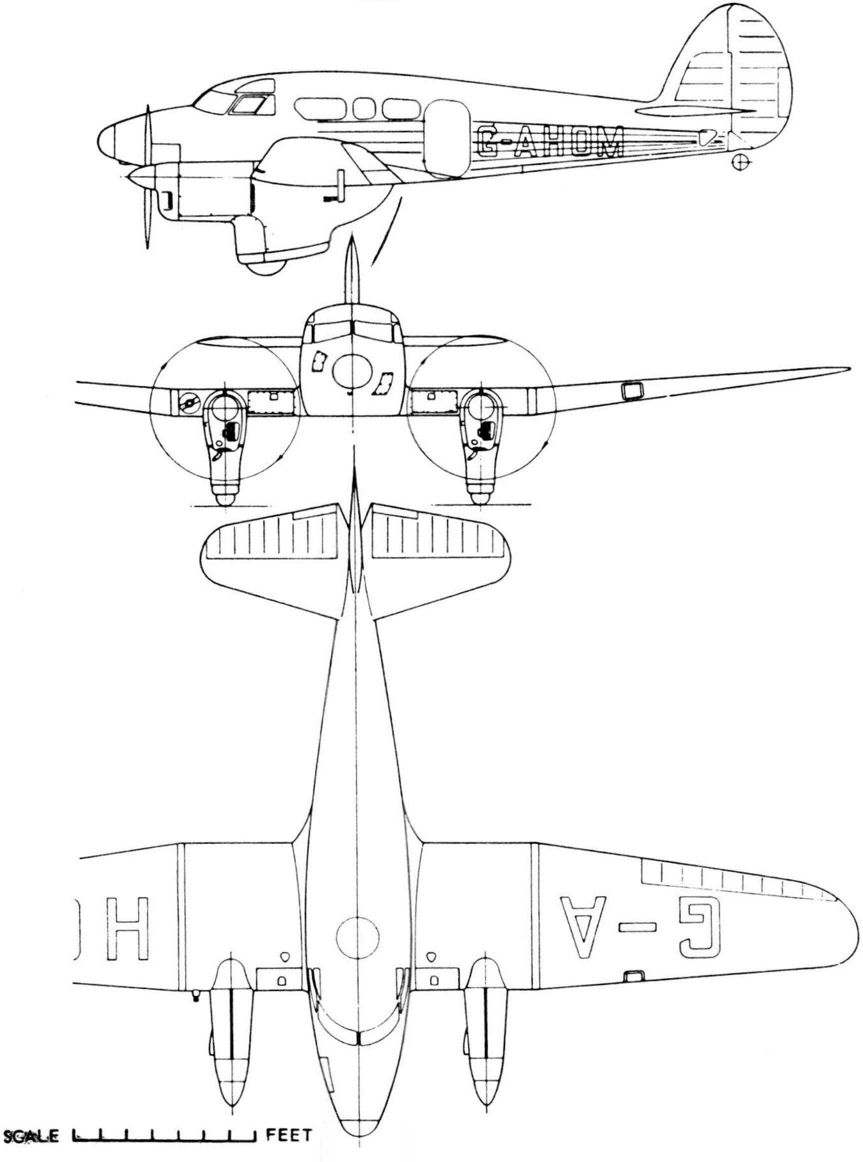

G-AHOM
G-A
H
SCALE FEET

Mew Gull E.3H

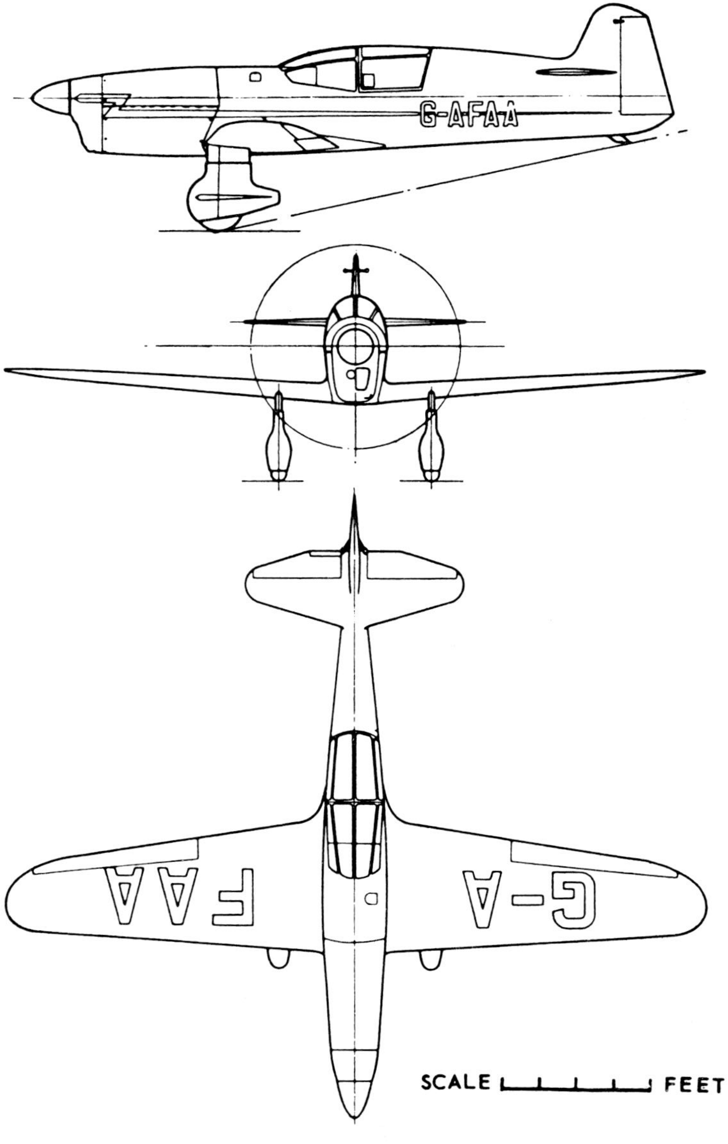

G-AFAA
G-A
FAA
SCALE FEET

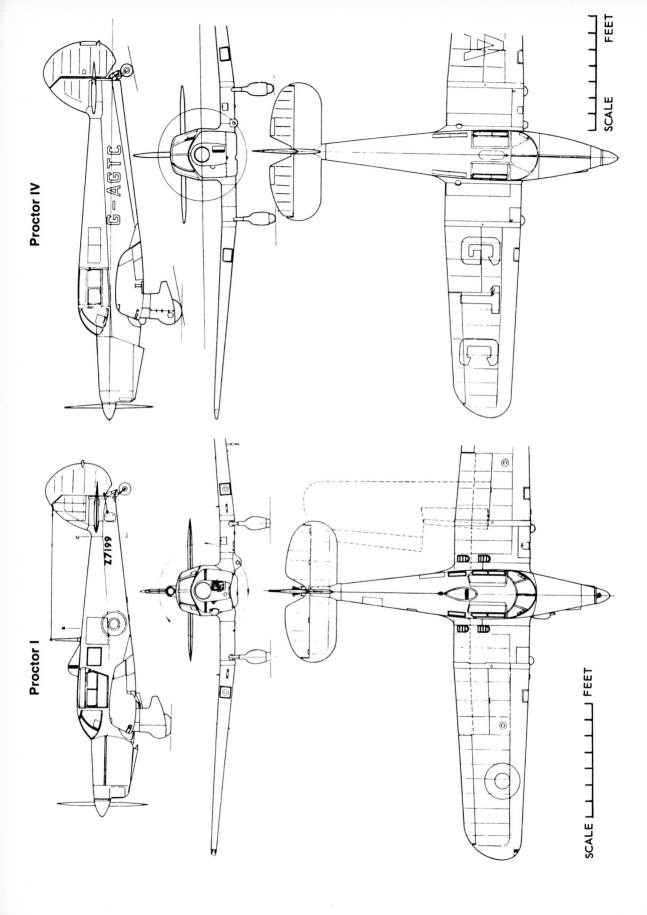

Proctor IV

Proctor I

SCALE FEET

SCALE FEET

Provost T Mk. 1

WV 492

SCALE ⌐⊢⊢⊢⊢⊢⊢⊢⊣ FEET

Prentice T Mk. 1

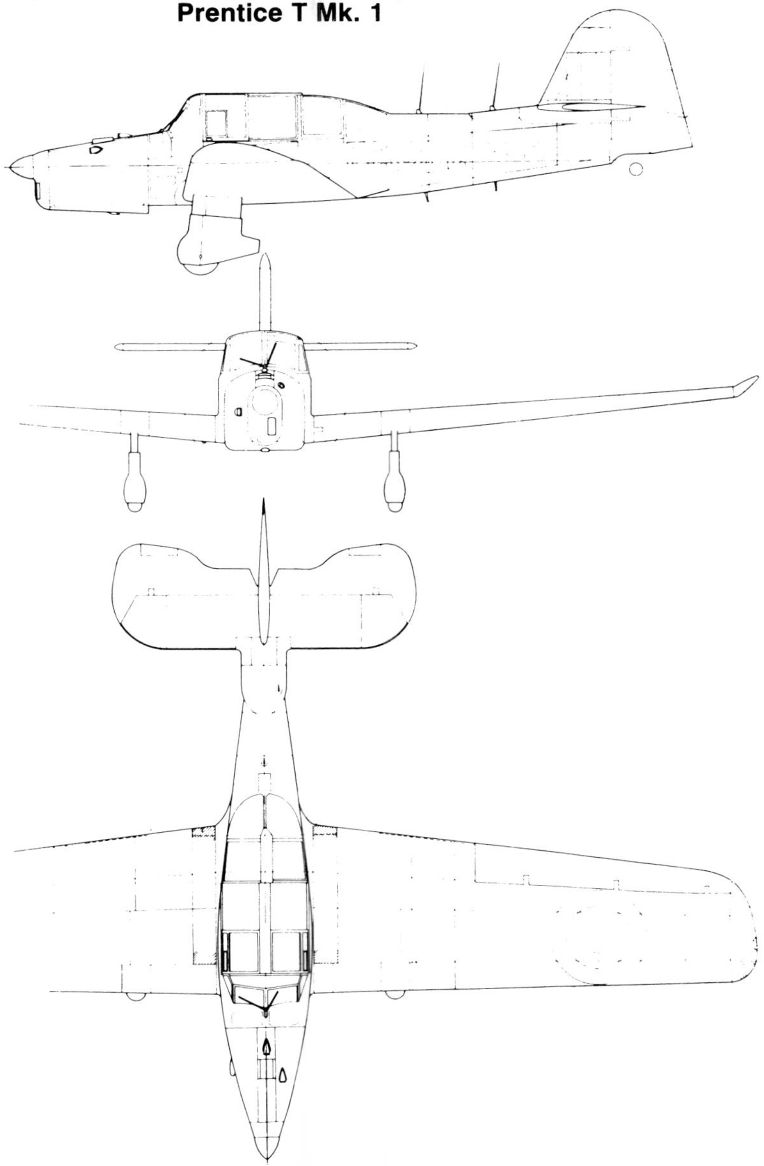

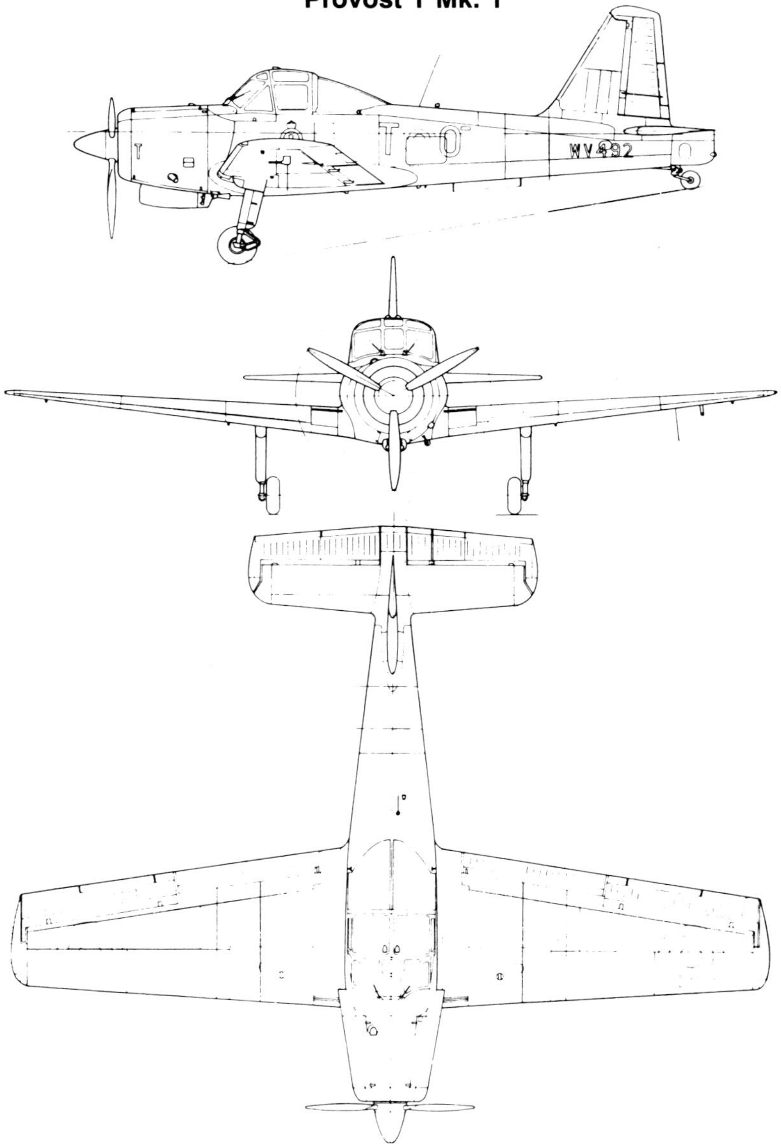

SCALE ⌐⊢⊢⊢⊢⊢⊢⊢⊣ FEET

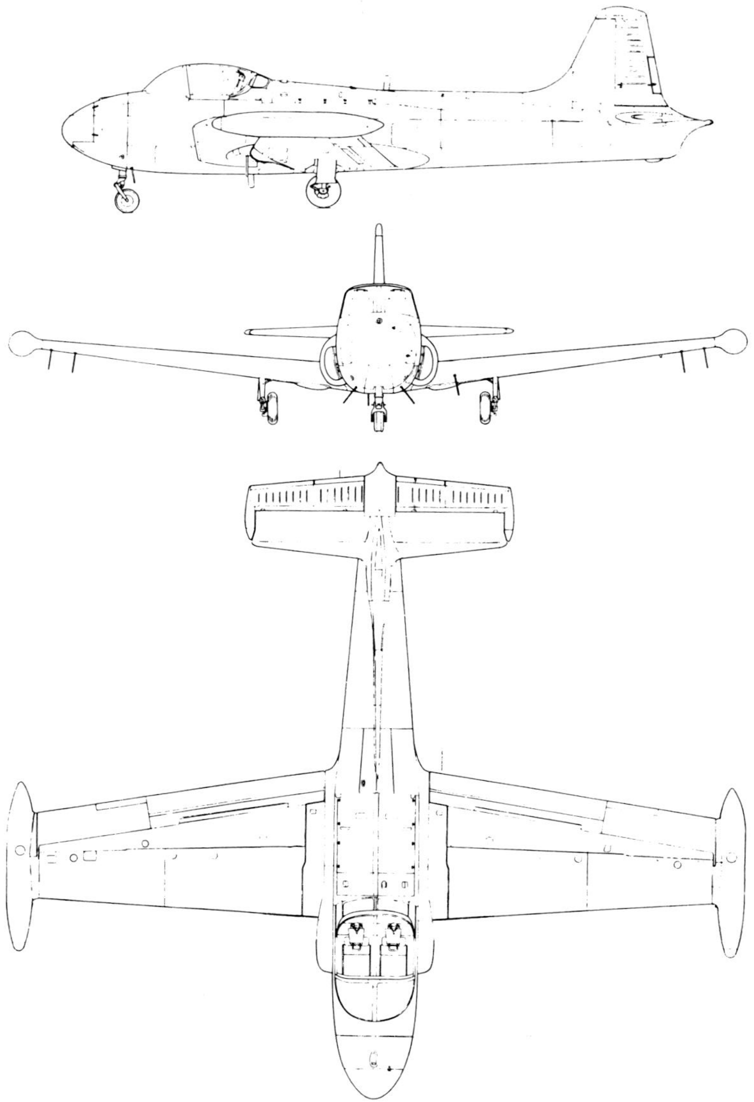

Prince

Jet Provost T Mk. 3

SCALE |___|___|___|___|___| FEET

SCALE |___|___|___|___|___| FEET

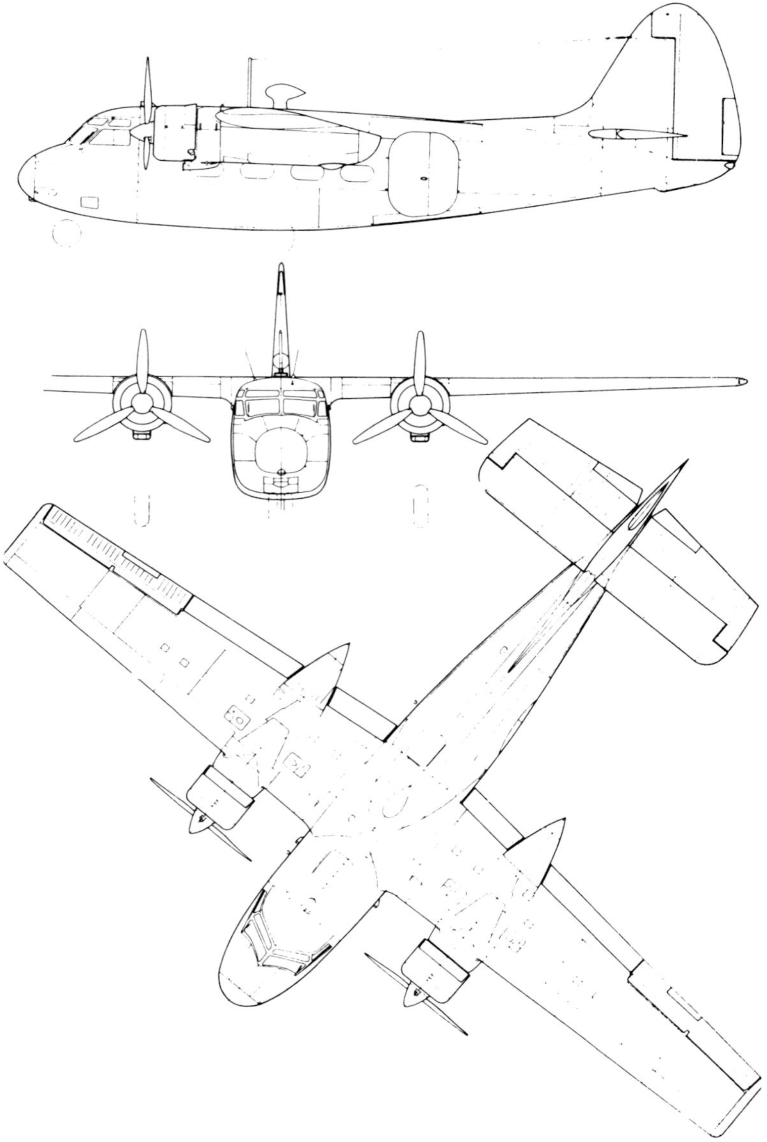

Sea Prince T Mk. 1

Pembroke and President

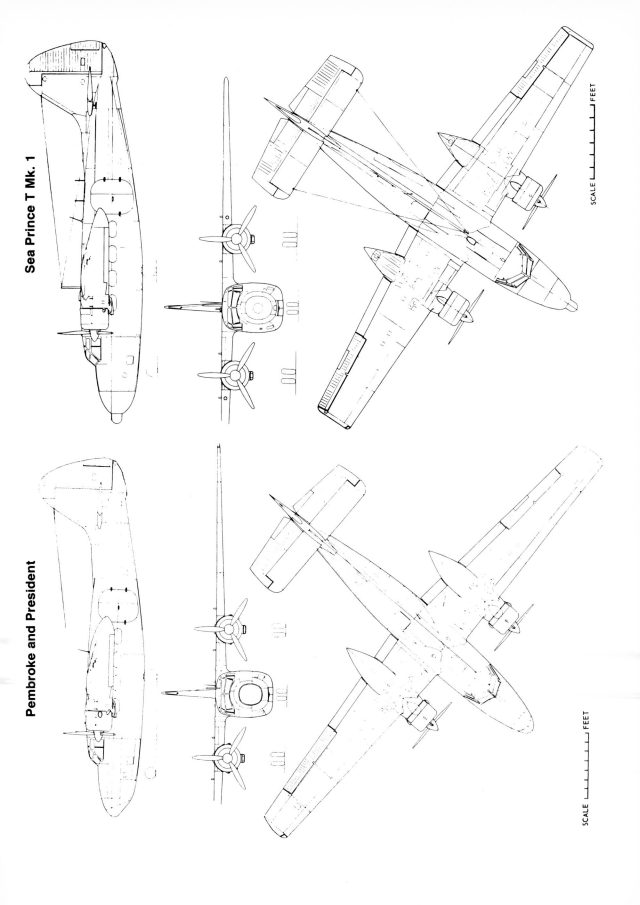

SCALE |⌐⊤⊤⊤⊤⊤⊤⊤⊤| FEET

SCALE |⌐⊤⊤⊤⊤⊤⊤⊤⊤| FEET

H107

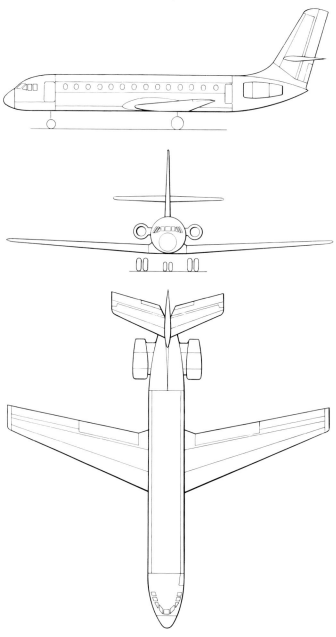

INDEX